Cisco Networking Academy Program:
Engineering Journal and Workbook
Volume I, Second Edition

Cisco Systems, Inc.

Cisco Networking Academy Program

Cisco Press

Cisco Press
201 West 103rd Street
Indianapolis, IN 46290 USA

Cisco Networking Academy Program:
Engineering Journal and Workbook
Volume I, Second Edition

Cisco Systems, Inc.

Cisco Networking Academy Program

201 West 103rd Street, Indianapolis, IN 46290

Published by:
Cisco Press
201 West 103rd Street
Indianapolis, IN 46290 USA

Printed in the United States of America   1 2 3 4 5 6 7 8 9 0

ISBN: 1-58713-026-2

Trademark Acknowledgments

All terms mentioned in this book that are known to be trademarks or service marks have been appropriately capitalized. Cisco Press or Cisco Systems, Inc., cannot attest to the accuracy of this information. Use of a term in this book should not be regarded as affecting the validity of any trademark or service mark.

Warning and Disclaimer

This book is designed to provide information on networking fundamentals. Every effort has been made to make this book as complete and as accurate as possible, but no warranty or fitness is implied.

The information is provided on an as-is basis. The author, Cisco Press, and Cisco Systems, Inc., shall have neither liability nor responsibility to any person or entity with respect to any loss or damages arising from the information contained in this book or from the use of the discs or programs that may accompany it.

The opinions expressed in this book belong to the author and are not necessarily those of Cisco Systems, Inc.

Feedback Information

At Cisco Press, our goal is to create in-depth technical books of the highest quality and value. Each book is crafted with care and precision, undergoing rigorous development that involves the unique expertise of members from the professional technical community.

Readers' feedback is a natural continuation of this process. If you have any comments regarding how we could improve the quality of this book, or otherwise alter it to better suit your needs, you can contact us at feedback@ciscopress.com. Please make sure to include the book title and ISBN in your message.

We greatly appreciate your assistance.

Publisher	*John Wait*
Executive Editor	*Carl Lindholm*
Cisco Systems Program Manager	*Bob Anstey*
Managing Editor	*Patrick Kanouse*
Senior Project Editor	*Sheri Replin*
Product Manager	*Shannon Gross*

Table of Contents

Preface

Since 1997, the Cisco Networking Academy Program has instituted an e-learning model that integrates the multimedia delivery of a networking curriculum with testing, performance-based skills assessment, evaluation, and reporting through a Web interface. The Cisco Networking Academy curriculum goes beyond traditional computer-based instruction by helping students develop practical networking knowledge and skills in a hands-on environment. In a lab setting that closely corresponds to a real networking environment, students work with the architecture and infrastructure pieces of networking technology. As a result, students learn the principles and practices of networking technology.

The Cisco Networking Academy Program provides in-depth and meaningful networking content, which is being used by Regional and Local Academies to teach students around the world by utilizing the curriculum to integrate networking instruction into the classroom. The focus of the Networking Academy program is on the integration of a Web-based network curriculum into the learning environment. This element is addressed through intensive staff development for instructors and innovative classroom materials and approaches to instruction, which are provided by Cisco. The participating educators are provided with resources, the means of remote access to online support, and the knowledge base for the effective classroom integration of the Cisco Networking Academy curriculum into the classroom learning environment. As a result, the Networking Academy program provides the means for the dynamic exchange of information by providing a suite of services that redefine the way instructional resources are disseminated, resulting in a many-to-many interactive and collaborative network of teachers and students functioning to meet diverse educational needs.

The Networking Academy curriculum is especially exciting to educators and students because the courseware is interactive. Because of the growing use of interactive technologies, the curriculum is an exciting new way to convey instruction with new interactive technologies that allow instructors and trainers to mix a number of media, including audio, video, text, numerical data, and graphics. Consequently, students can select different media from the computer screen and tweak their instructional content to meet their instructional needs, and educators have the option of either designing their own environment for assessment or selecting from the applicable assessments.

Finally, by developing a curriculum that recognizes the changing classroom and workforce demographics, the globalization of the economy, changing workforce knowledge and skill requirements, and the role of technology in education, the Cisco Networking Academy Program supports national educational goals for K-12 education. As support for the Networking Academy program, Cisco Press published this book, *Cisco Networking Academy Program: Engineering Journal and Workbook*, Volume I, Second Edition, as a further complement to the curriculum used in the Cisco Networking Academy Program.

Introduction

Cisco Networking Academy Program: Engineering Journal and Workbook, Volume I, Second Edition, is designed to act as a supplement to your classroom and laboratory experience with the Cisco Networking Academy Program, whose curriculum is designed to empower you to enter employment or further education and training in the computer networking field.

This tool is designed to further train you beyond the online training materials that you have already used in this program, along with the topics pertaining to the Cisco Certified Network Associate (CCNA) exam. This book closely follows the style and format that Cisco has incorporated into the curriculum. In addition, this book follows the two-semester curriculum model that has already been developed for the Cisco Networking Academy Program. The *Engineering Journal and Workbook* provides you with additional exercises and activities that help to reinforce your learning. We also included writing opportunities that help you learn to establish and keep an engineering journal.

We recommend that you keep a technical or engineering journal. Typically, a journal is a paper-bound composition book in which pages are not added or subtracted, but dated. The types of journal entries most applicable for Networking Academy students include daily reflections, troubleshooting details, lab procedures and observations, equipment logs, hardware and software notes, and router configurations. Because the journal becomes much more important as you do more network design and installation work, good habits can be developed by starting with a journal on the first day of the first semester. In this book, you are asked to keep your journal on a daily basis.

Chapter 1   Computer Basics

Introduction

Three reasons why it is important to able to recognize and name the major components of a PC are

- Computers are important network-building devices.
- Many networking devices are themselves special-purpose computers, with many of the same parts as "normal" PCs.
- In order for you to view the online curriculum, your own computer must be in working order, which means that you might need to occasionally troubleshoot simple problems in your computer's hardware and software.

Concept Questions

Demonstrate your knowledge of these concepts by answering the questions in the Engineering Journal space provided.

- **The transistor and the integrated circuit made modern computers possible. Explain why.**

- **If your computer doesn't power up, what steps might you take to identify and correct the problem?**

- After you set up the PC hardware, you must configure its software. You must complete the following tasks in order to be able to view the curriculum.

- **Explain how to**
    Select the NIC card
    Set the correct IP address
    Adjust the display (if necessary)
    Install and set up the browser

Engineering Journal
In the space provided, answer the Concept Questions.

_____

_____

_____

_____

_____

_____

_____

Engineering Journal (Continued)

Vocabulary Exercise Chapter 1   Name: _____

Date: _____   Class: _____

Define the following terms as completely as you can. Use the online Chapter 1 or the *Cisco Systems Networking Academy: First-Year Companion Guide*, Second Edition, material for help.

ASCII (American Standard Code for Information Interchange)

_____

_____

Back Plane

_____

_____

Back Plane Components

_____

_____

Binary

_____

_____

Bits

_____

_____

Bus

_____

_____

Bytes

_____

_____

Capacitor

_____

_____

CD-ROM drive

_____

_____

CPU

_____

_____

Expansion slots

_____

_____

Floppy disk drive

_____

_____

Hard disk drive

_____

_____

Integrated circuit

_____

_____

Light emitting diodes (LEDs)

_____

_____

Local-area networks (LANs)

_____

_____

Microprocessor

_____

_____

Monitor connector

_____

_____

Motherboard

_____

_____

Mouse port

_____

_____

Network

_____

_____

Network card

_____

_____

NIC (network interface card)

_____

_____

Parallel port

_____

_____

PC components

_____

_____

Personal Computer Subsystems

_____

_____

Power cord

_____

_____

Power supply

_____

_____

Printed circuit boards (PCBs)

_____

_____

Protocol

_____

_____

RAM

_____

_____

Resistor

_____

_____

ROM

_____

_____

Serial port

_____

_____

Small, Discrete Components

_____

_____

Solder

_____

_____

Sound card

_____

_____

System unit

_____

_____

Throughput

_____

_____

Transistor

_____

_____

Video card

_____

_____

Wide-area networks (WANs)

_____

_____

Focus Questions   Name: _____

Date: _____   **Class:** _____

1. What are the major components of a PC?

_____
_____
_____
_____

2. What is the information flow in an idealized computer?

_____
_____
_____
_____

3. What is the relationship of NICs to PCs?

_____
_____
_____
_____

4. Compare PC components with laptop components.

_____
_____
_____
_____

5. What is data throughput and how does it relate to digital bandwidth?

_____
_____
_____
_____

6. Why are there different bandwidths?

_____
_____

7. What units measure the quantity of information?

_____
_____

8. How do binary numbers represent alphanumeric data?

_____
_____

CCNA Exam Review Questions

The following questions help you review for the CCNA exam. Answers are found in Appendix A, "Answers to the CCNA Exam Review Questions."

1. Which of the following best defines networking?
    a. A set of rules or procedures that are either widely used or officially specified
    b. A connection of computers, printers, and other devices for the purpose of communication
    c. A set of rules that govern how computer workstations exchange information
    d. A device connected to a computer to provide auxiliary functions

2. What is a connection of computers, printers, and other devices for purpose of communication?
    a. Peripheral
    b. Network
    c. Mainframe
    d. Protocol

3. Which of the following terms is used in computing to refer to physical parts or equipment?
    a. Hardware
    b. Software
    c. Protocol
    d. Network

4. Which of the following terms is used in computing to refer to programs or applications?
    a. Hardware
    b. Software
    c. Peripheral
    d. Network

5. Which of the following refers to devices connected to a computer to provide auxiliary functions such as printing, added disk space, scanning, or CD-ROM?
    a. Protocol
    b. Software
    c. Peripheral
    d. Network

6. Why are individual PCs not efficient or cost effective for business applications?
    a. Individual PC use requires businesses to duplicate equipment and resources.
    b. It is difficult for businesses to communicate quickly or efficiently using individual PCs.
    c. It is difficult to provide management for operating individual PCs.
    d. All of the above.

7. What is a stand-alone computer?
    a. A computer that manages data efficiently
    b. A computer that shares files and printers with other computers
    c. A computer that operates independently from other computers
    d. A computer that has a different operating system

8. What kind of computer operates independently from other computers?
    a. Mainframe
    b. PC
    c. Mac
    d. Stand-alone

9. Why did stand-alone computers become an inefficient and ineffective way for businesses to operate?
    a. Businesses had to duplicate equipment and resources.
    b. It was difficult to communicate quickly or efficiently using stand-alone computers.
    c. It was difficult to provide management for operating stand-alone computers.
    d. All of the above.

10. What does the term *protocol* mean in computing terms?
    a. A tool that lets Macintosh and PC computers communicate with each other
    b. A universal translator that allows different kinds of computers to share data
    c. A description of a set of rules and conventions that govern how devices on a network exchange information
    d. The language that all the computers on a network must use to communicate with each other

11. Which of the following best defines *protocol*?
    a. A formal description of a set of rules and conventions
    b. A device connected to a computer to provide auxiliary functions
    c. A group of people who are assigned to work as a team
    d. The connection of computers, printers, routers and switches

12. What is a formal description of a set of rules and conventions called?
    a. Peripheral
    b. Protocol
    c. Standard
    d. Network

13. Why are protocols important?
    a. By setting rules, they allow different types of computers to talk to each other.
    b. By consolidating the industry, they save companies money.
    c. By forming electronic islands, they bypass the sneaker net.
    d. By using common carriers, they manage data efficiently.

14. What must all computers on a network be able to do for the network to operate properly?
    a. Print to a local printer
    b. Connect to a telephone line
    c. Use CD-ROMs
    d. Speak the same language

15. A protocol allows which of the following to be linked into a network?
    a. Only PC terminals and workstations
    b. Only Macintosh computers and peripherals
    c. Only PCs to a mainframe
    d. Any type of computer terminal or workstation

Engineering Journal (Continued)

Chapter 2   The OSI Model

Introduction

The OSI reference model is a descriptive network scheme whose standards ensure greater compatibility and interoperability between various types of network technologies. Further, the OSI reference model is a way of illustrating how information travels through networks. It is a conceptual framework specifying the network functions that occur at each layer. The OSI model describes how information or data makes its way from application programs (such as spreadsheets) through a network medium (such as wires) to another application program located on another computer on a network.

Concept Questions

Demonstrate your knowledge of these concepts by answering the following questions in the space provided.

The ISO recognized the need to create a network model that would help vendors create interoperable network implementations and released the OSI reference model in 1984.

- The OSI reference model is a descriptive network scheme whose standards ensure greater compatibility and interoperability between various types of network technologies. **Why is such a standard necessary?**

- The OSI reference model organizes network distinct functions into seven numbered layers: **Briefly describe what each layer does.**

Layer 7: The application layer _____

Layer 6: The presentation layer _____

Layer 5: The session layer _____

Layer 4: The transport layer _____

Layer 3: The network layer _____

Layer 2: The data link layer _____

Layer 1: The physical layer _____

Engineering Journal
In the space provided, answer the Concept Questions.

_____
_____
_____
_____
_____
_____
_____
_____
_____
_____
_____
_____
_____
_____
_____
_____
_____
_____
_____
_____
_____
_____
_____
_____
_____
_____
_____
_____
_____
_____
_____
_____
_____
_____
_____
_____
_____
_____
_____
_____
_____
_____
_____

Vocabulary Exercise Chapter 2   **Name:** _____

Date: _____   **Class:** _____

Define the following terms as completely as you can. Use the online Chapter 2 or the
Cisco Systems Networking Academy: First-Year Companion Guide, Second Edition,
material for help.

Datagram

_____
_____
_____

Encapsulation

_____
_____
_____

Frame

_____
_____
_____

Layer 1: Physical

_____
_____
_____

Layer 2: Data Link

_____
_____
_____

Layer 3: Network

_____
_____
_____

Layer 4: Transport

_____
_____
_____

Layer 5: Session

_____
_____
_____

Layer 6: Presentation

_____
_____
_____

Layer 7: Application

_____
_____
_____

Packet

_____
_____
_____

Peer-to-peer

_____
_____
_____

Segment

_____
_____
_____

TCP/IP

_____
_____
_____

TCP/IP Application Layer

_____
_____
_____

TCP/IP Internet Layer

_____
_____
_____

TCP/IP Network

_____
_____
_____

Focus Questions   **Name:** _____

Date: _____   **Class:** _____

1. Briefly describe six reasons why a layered network model is used in Internetworking?

    _____   _____
    _____   _____
    _____   _____

2. From memory, list the seven layers of the OSI model and briefly describe their function.

    Layer 7 _____
    Layer 6 _____
    Layer 5 _____
    Layer 4 _____
    Layer 3 _____
    Layer 2 _____
    Layer 1 _____

3. What is meant by the term *Peer-to-Peer Communication*?

    _____
    _____
    _____

4. Briefly describe the process of data encapsulation using the following terms: data, segment, packet, frame, bits.

    _____
    _____
    _____
    _____
    _____
    _____

5. Describe the information that is added at the data as it is encapsulated in the transport, network, and data link layers.

    _____
    _____
    _____
    _____
    _____
    _____

6. What is the OSI reference model?

_____

_____

_____

7. Will networks that are built following the OSI model be identical?

_____

_____

_____

8. What process does the OSI model describe?

_____

_____

_____

9. Define *medium*.

_____

_____

_____

10. What is the importance of the TCP/IP model?

_____

_____

_____

11. How does the OSI model compare with the TCP/IP model?

_____

_____

_____

CCNA Exam Review Questions
The following questions help you prepare for the CCNA exam. Answers are found in Appendix A, "Answers to the CCNA Exam Review Questions."

1. Which of the following best defines standards?
    a. A set of rules or procedures that are either widely used or officially specified
    b. A connection of computers, printers, and other devices for purposes of communication
    c. A set of rules that govern how computer workstations exchange information
    d. A device connected to a computer to provide auxiliary functions

2. What is the OSI model?
    a. A conceptual framework that specifies how information travels through networks
    b. A model that describes how data makes its way from one application program to another through a network
    c. A conceptual framework that specifies which network functions occur at each layer
    d. All of the above

3. As described by the OSI model, how does data move across a network?
    a. Directly from each layer at one computer to the corresponding layers at another computer
    b. Through wires connecting each layer from computer to computer
    c. Down through the layers at one computer and up through the layers at another
    d. Through layers in wires between computers

4. Which best defines the function of the lower layers (called the media layers) of the OSI model?
    a. Provide for the accurate delivery of data between computers
    b. Convert data into the ones and zeros that a computer understands
    c. Receive data from peripheral devices
    d. Control the physical delivery of messages over the network

5. Which of the following describes the host layers of the OSI model?
    a. Control the physical delivery of messages over the network
    b. Make up the lower layers in the OSI model
    c. Contain data that is more like ones and zeros than like human language
    d. Provide for accurate delivery of data between computers

6. Which of the following best describes the purpose of the physical layer?
    a. Defines the electrical, mechanical, procedural, and functional specifications for activating, maintaining, and deactivating the link between end systems
    b. Provides reliable transit of data across a physical link
    c. Provides connectivity and path selection between two end systems
    d. Establishes, manages, and terminates sessions between applications and manages data exchange between presentation layer entities

7. Which layer of the OSI model is concerned with physical addressing, network topology, line discipline, error notification, ordered delivery of frames, and flow control?
    a. Physical layer
    b. Data link layer
    c. Transport layer
    d. Network layer

8. Which layer of the OSI model provides connectivity and path selection between two end systems where routing occurs?
    a. Physical layer
    b. Data link layer
    c. Network layer
    d. Transport layer

9. Which layer of the OSI model is responsible for reliable network communication between end nodes and provides mechanisms for the establishment, maintenance, and termination of virtual circuits, transport fault detection and recovery, and information flow control?
    a. Physical layer
    b. Data link layer
    c. Network layer
    d. Transport layer

10. Which layer of the OSI model establishes, manages, and terminates sessions between applications and manages data exchange between presentation layer entities?
    a. Transport layer
    b. Session layer
    c. Presentation layer
    d. Application layer

11. Which layer of the OSI model ensures that information sent by the application layer of one system will be readable by the application layer of another system, is concerned with the data structures used by programs, and negotiates data transfer syntax for the application layer?
    a. Transport layer
    b. Session layer
    c. Presentation layer
    d. Application layer

12. Which layer of the OSI model identifies and establishes the availability of intended communication partners, synchronizes cooperating applications, and establishes agreement on procedures for error recovery and control of data integrity?
    a. Transport layer
    b. Session layer
    c. Presentation layer
    d. Application layer

13. Which of the following best defines encapsulation?
    a. Segmenting data so it flows uninterrupted through the network
    b. Compressing data so it moves faster
    c. Moving data in groups so it stays together
    d. Wrapping of data in a particular protocol header

14. What analogy might be used to describe encapsulation?
    a. Encapsulation is like a blueprint for building a car.
    b. Encapsulation is like sending a package through the mail.
    c. Encapsulation is like building a fence around your backyard.
    d. Encapsulation is like driving a car to the store to buy groceries.

15. What is a data packet?
    a. Logically grouped units of information
    b. Transmission devices
    c. Auxiliary function provided by peripherals
    d. Virtual circuits

Engineering Journal (Continued)

Chapter 3   **Local-Area Networks**

Introduction

Local-area networks (LANs) are high-speed, low-error data networks that cover a relatively small geographic area (up to a few thousand meters). LANs connect workstations, peripherals, terminals, and other devices in a single building or another geographically limited area. LANs provide multiple-connected desktop devices (usually PCs) with access to high-bandwidth media. LANs connect computers and services to a common Layer 1 media.

Concept Questions

Demonstrate your knowledge of these concepts by answering the following questions in the space provided.

- The network operates within a building or floor of a building. **What are the major characteristics of a LAN?**
- **What are the major components of the average LAN?**

Engineering Journal
In the space provided, answer the Concept Questions.

_____
_____
_____
_____
_____
_____
_____
_____
_____
_____
_____
_____
_____
_____
_____
_____
_____
_____
_____
_____
_____
_____
_____

Engineering Journal (Continued)

Vocabulary Exercise Chapter 3   Name: _____

Date: _____   **Class:** _____

Define the following terms as completely as you can. Use the online Chapter 3 or the
Cisco Systems Networking Academy: First-Year Companion Guide, Second Edition,
material for help.

AUI

_____
_____
_____

Bridge

_____
_____
_____

Hub

_____
_____
_____

IEEE 802.3

_____
_____
_____

LAN

_____
_____
_____

MAC address

_____
_____
_____

MAU

_____
_____
_____

Media

_____

_____

_____

NIC

_____

_____

_____

RAM

_____

_____

_____

ROM

_____

_____

_____

Router

_____

_____

_____

Switch

_____

_____

_____

Focus Questions   **Name:** _____

Date: _____   **Class:** _____

1. What are the functions and OSI layer of
    Computers _____   _____
    Clients _____   _____
    Servers _____   _____
    Relational databases _____   _____
    Printers _____   _____

2. What is the purpose and OSI layer of network interface cards (NICs) in a LAN?

    _____
    _____
    _____
    _____

3. What is the appearance and OSI layer of media in a LAN?

    _____
    _____
    _____
    _____

4. What is the symbol and OSI layer of repeater, as it applies to a LAN?

    _____
    _____
    _____
    _____

5. What is the function and OSI layer of hub, as it applies to a LAN?

    _____
    _____
    _____
    _____

6. What is the symbol and OSI layer of bridge, as it applies to a LAN?

    _____
    _____
    _____
    _____

7. What is the function and OSI layer of a switch on a LAN?

    _____
    _____
    _____
    _____

8. What is the appearance and OSI layer of router on a LAN?

    _____

    _____

    _____

    _____

9. What is the symbol and OSI layer of a cloud?

    _____

    _____

    _____

    _____

10. What is the function and OSI layer of network segments?

    _____

    _____

    _____

    _____

CCNA Exam Review Questions
The following questions help you prepare for the CCNA Exam. Answers are found in Appendix A, "Answers to the CCNA Exam Review Questions."

1. What business problem resulting from the proliferation of stand-alone computers did networks solve?
    a. Inability to communicate and lack of management
    b. Losses due to lack of business by common carriers
    c. Inefficient use of information technology professionals
    d. Increasing level of electromagnetic interference

2. What did early networks allow?
    a. Common carriers to finally make a profit
    b. Workers to copy files onto floppies and then carry the disks to a coworker's PC to print
    c. The duplication of resources to expand
    d. The easy and efficient sharing of files and printers

3. Which of the following is *not* a problem that networking helped solve?
    a. Lack of network management
    b. Lack of new hardware and software products
    c. Duplication of equipment and resources
    d. Inability to communicate efficiently

4. Why is it desirable to network?
    a. Don't have to duplicate equipment and resources
    b. Makes it easy to communicate quickly or efficiently using stand-alone computers
    c. Makes it easy to provide management for operating stand-alone computers
    d. All of the above

5. Why is networking a variety of networks together difficult?
    a. People try to network different types of computer systems together.
    b. Emerging network technologies use different hardware and software specifications.
    c. Incompatibility due to hardware changes.
    d. Computer designers try to make their own protocols and they are incompatible.

6. Why are networking standards needed?
    a. Many networks now cover wide geographic areas.
    b. Technologies must be compatible to allow communication.
    c. Hardware and software are continually being redesigned.
    d. LANs, MANs, and WANs use different kinds of equipment.

7. Why did networks experience problems in the mid-1980s?
   a. Many new network technologies were incompatible.
   b. Employees preferred sneaker net.
   c. Common carriers went bankrupt.
   d. Everyone used the same hardware and software.

8. Why did using different hardware and software cause problems after networks were established?
   a. Networks cannot be formed if some people have Macs and others have PCs.
   b. Different hardware and software did not provide auxiliary functions for the users.
   c. Different hardware and software implementations used in the new technologies were incompatible.
   d. Each department or business was not able to act as an electronic island; instead, they were forced to work together.

9. What is a LAN?
   a. A network that connects workstations, terminals, and other devices in a geographically limited area.
   b. A network that connects workstations, terminals, and other devices in a metropolitan area.
   c. A network that serves users across a broad geographic area and often uses transmission devices provided by a common carrier.
   d. A network that covers a larger area than a MAN.

10. Which of the following best describes a LAN?
    a. A data network connecting workstations, peripherals, terminals, and other devices in a single building or other geographically limited area.
    b. A data network that connects workstations, peripherals, terminals, and other devices across a broad geographic area.
    c. A data network that connects workstations, peripherals, terminals, and other devices across a metropolitan area.
    d. A data network that connects workstations, peripherals, terminals and other devices within a single building.

11. What is a network that connects computer equipment in a single building called?
    a. LAN
    b. WAN
    c. MAN
    d. DCN

12. A segment of a network is
    a. A section consisting of several interconnected computers, such as a LAN
    b. A physical wire, such as CAT 5 cable of fiber optic cable
    c. A single PC that is part of a LAN
    d. A part of a network that has been temporarily disconnected

Engineering Journal (Continued)

Chapter 4   Layer 1: Electronics and Signals

Introduction

Electricity is a fact of modern life. We use it to perform a variety of tasks. It is brought to our homes, schools, and offices by power lines that carry it in the form of *alternating current (AC)*. Another type of current, called *direct current (DC)*, is the current found in a flashlight, car battery, and on the motherboard of a computer.

It is important to understand the difference between these two types of current flow. Direct current flows at a constant value when circuits are turned on. Alternating current rises and falls in current values as it is manufactured by power companies.

Once it reaches our homes, schools, and offices, electricity is carried to appliances and machines via wires concealed in walls, floors, and ceilings. Consequently, inside these buildings, AC powerline noise is all around us. If not properly addressed, powerline noise can present problems for a network.

In fact, as you discover the more you work with networks, AC line noise coming from a nearby video monitor or hard disk drive can be enough to create errors in a computer system. It does this by burying the desired signals and preventing a computer's logic gates from detecting the leading and trailing edges of the square signal waves. This problem can be further compounded when a computer has a poor ground connection.

The third type of electricity is *static electricity*. This most damaging uncontrollable form of electricity must be dealt with in order to protect sensitive electronic equipment. Such static discharges can destroy semiconductors and data in a seemingly random fashion as they shoot through a computer like bullets. As it can with problems related to AC line noise, good grounding helps solve problems that arise from electrostatic discharge.

Concept Questions

Demonstrate your knowledge of these concepts by answering the following questions in the space provided.

- Each wire in a cable can act like an antenna. When this happens, the wire actually absorbs electrical signals from other wires in the cable and from electrical sources outside the cable. If the resulting electrical noise reaches a high-enough level, it can become difficult for NIC cards to discriminate the noise from the data signal. When electrical noise on the cable originates from signals on other wires in the cable, this is known as crosstalk. **How can you minimize crosstalk?**

- To ensure optimal performance, it is important for the network media to carry the signal from one device to another with as little degradation as possible. In networking, several factors can cause the signal to degrade. Some of these factors are internal, while others are external. **Name some of the factors that can cause a signal to degrade and how to correct the problem.**

- Inside copper wires, factors such as opposition to the flow of electrons (resistance), opposition to changes in voltage (capacitance), and opposition to changes in current (inductance), can cause signals to degrade. External sources of electrical impulses that can attack the quality of electrical signals on the cable include lighting, electrical motors, and radio systems. These types of interference are referred to as electromagnetic interference, or EMI, and radio frequency interference, or RFI. **How can you protect your network from RFI?**

Engineering Journal
In the space provided, answer the Concept Questions.

_____
_____
_____
_____
_____
_____
_____
_____
_____
_____
_____
_____
_____
_____
_____
_____
_____
_____
_____
_____
_____
_____
_____
_____
_____
_____
_____
_____
_____
_____
_____
_____

Vocabulary Exercise Chapter 4   Name: _____

Date: _____   **Class:** _____

Define the following terms as completely as you can. Use the online Chapter 4 or the
Cisco Systems Networking Academy: First-Year Companion Guide, Second Edition,
material for help.

Alternating current (AC)

_____
_____

AM (amplitude modulation)

_____
_____

Analog transmission

_____
_____

Attenuation

_____
_____

Circuits

_____
_____

Conductor

_____
_____

Digital signal

_____
_____

Direct current (DC)

_____
_____

Electricity

_____
_____

Electrons

_____
_____

Electrostatic discharge (ESD)

_____

_____

FM (frequency modulation)

_____

_____

Impedance

_____

_____

Latency

_____

_____

Multimeter

_____

_____

Neutrons

_____

_____

Oscilloscope

_____

_____

PM (phase modulation)

_____

_____

Propagation

_____

_____

Protons

_____

_____

Focus Questions   **Name:** _____

Date: _____   **Class:** _____

1. What are some examples of electrical insulators?

_____

_____

2. What are some examples of electrical conductors?

_____

_____

3. What are some examples of semiconductors?

_____

_____

4. What is silicon made of? Is it an insulator, conductor, or semiconductor?

_____

_____

5. Do semiconductors allow the amount of electricity to be controlled?

_____

_____

6. When does voltage occur?

_____

_____

7. What is it called when static, or resting, electrons move and a flow of charges is created?

_____

_____

8. What is the abbreviation for amps?

_____

_____

9. What is the abbreviation for resistance?

_____

_____

10. What is the difference between AC and DC?

_____

_____

11. How do you measure impedance? What is its abbreviation?

_____

_____

12. What three components are necessary to make up a circuit and how do they allow the control of current?

_____

_____

13. What equipment do you use to graph electrical waves, pulses, and patterns?

_____

_____

14. What are some of the characteristics of an analog signal?

_____

_____

15. What is the basic building block of information on a data network?

_____

_____

16. What are the five sources of noise that can affect a bit on a wire?

_____

_____

17. At what speed do modern networks typically work?

_____

_____

CCNA Exam Review Questions
The following questions help you review for the CCNA exam. Answers are found in the section, "Answers to the CCNA Exam Review Questions."

1. Which of the following correctly describes the type of signal carried by the network media?
    a. Coaxial cable carries pulses of light.
    b. Unshielded twisted-pair cable carries impedance signals.
    c. Shielded twisted-pair cable carries electrical impulses.
    d. Fiber-optic cable carries electrical impulses.

2. Which network media carries pulses of light?
    a. Coaxial cable
    b. Fiber-optic cable
    c. Unshielded twisted-pair cable
    d. Shielded twisted-pair cable

3. Which of the following is an external source of degradation of the signal on cabling?
    a. EMI caused by electrical motors
    b. RFI caused by light leakage
    c. Impedance caused by radio systems
    d. RFI caused by lighting

4. Which of the following describes cabling signal degradation by an external source?
    a. Poor cabling shield connection
    b. RFI caused by radio systems
    c. EMI caused by twisting of wires
    d. Impedance caused by electrical motors

5. What is the cause of crosstalk?
    a. Cable wires that are too large in diameter
    b. Too much noise in a cable's data signal
    c. Electrical motors and lighting
    d. Electrical signals from other wires in a cable

6. How does crosstalk occur?
    a. Two wires are placed in close proximity to each other.
    b. NIC cards fail to discriminate the noise from the data signal.
    c. Electrical noise originates from signals on other wires in the cable.
    d. Wires in a cable absorb electrical impulses from sources outside the cable.

7. What is a cost-effective method of limiting cable signal degradation?
   a. Specify the maximum cable length between nodes.
   b. Increase the size of the conductors in the cabling.
   c. Improve the type of insulating material.
   d. Use a braid or foil covering on wires as a shield.

8. How can cable signal degradation be limited in a cost-effective way?
   a. Improve the type of insulating material.
   b. Place same-circuit wires close to each other.
   c. Use a braid or foil covering on wires as a shield.
   d. Increase the diameter of the conductor in the cabling.

9. What is cancellation in networking media?
   a. The magnetic fields of same-circuit wires cancel each other.
   b. External magnetic fields cancel the fields inside network cabling.
   c. Wires in the same circuit cancel each other's electrical current flow.
   d. Twisting wire pairs cancels the electrical impedance in the wires.

10. Which of the following describes cancellation in cabling?
    a. Wires in the same circuit cancel each other's electrical current flow.
    b. Twisting wire pairs provides self-shielding within the network media.
    c. The magnetic fields of wires on different electrical circuits cancel each other.
    d. External magnetic fields cancel the fields inside network cabling.

11. Which of the following describes impedance in networking media?
    a. Impedance involves resistance and reactance to current caused by signal degradation.
    b. Electrical components in the NIC cards create impedance on the networking media.
    c. Signal degradation causes impedance.
    d. Networking media impedance needs to match the NIC card electrical components.

12. When can impedance degrade the signal in networking media?
    a. When resistance opposes reactance
    b. When cable impedance does not match NIC card electrical components
    c. When networking media is not properly shielded from EMI/RFI interference
    d. When cancellation techniques are not employed

13. Which of the following best describes attenuation?
    a. The termination of a message
    b. The interception of a message
    c. The weakening of a message
    d. The ignoring of a message

14. How is data transmitted on a network?
    a. As hexadecimal code
    b. As ASCII text
    c. As 1s and 0s
    d. As voltage pulses

15. Which best describes the states of digital signals?
    a. Alphanumeric
    b. Octets
    c. On or off
    d. Yes or no

16. What does the binary number 1 correspond to in a digital signal?
    a. On
    b. One
    c. The letter *A*
    d. Off

17. What does the binary number 0 correspond to in a digital signal?
    a. On
    b. One
    c. The letter *A*
    d. Off

18. Which best describes a digital signal?
    a. A sine wave of normal shape and amplitude
    b. An electrical technique used to convey binary signals
    c. Language of computers with only two states, on and off, which are indicated by a series of voltage pulses
    d. Transmission sent by a transceiver back to a controller to let it know the collision circuitry is functional

19. How do computers recognize digital signals?
    a. They receive a broadcast signal from the network.
    b. They look for ARP requests that match their IP address.
    c. They monitor the network connection for modulations.
    d. They measure and compare the signals to a reference point.

20. What is the signal reference ground?
    a. Neutral contact point where the computer chassis and the network connection meet
    b. Point used by devices to measure and compare incoming digital signals to
    c. Device that the name server uses to send messages over the network
    d. Ground that prevents users from receiving shocks when power fails

21. What is the point used by a device to measure and compare incoming digital signals called?
    a. Input point
    b. Zero point
    c. Null reference setting
    d. Signal reference ground

22. How is the signal reference ground established?
    a. By connecting the ground wire to the network wire
    b. By connecting the network wire to the jumper connector
    c. By connecting the ground plane to the computer's cabinet
    d. By connecting the computer chassis to the network cable

23. What purpose does the computer chassis serve?
    a. Prevents electrical short circuits and electrical fires
    b. Signal reference ground and AC power line ground
    c. Amplifies digital signals
    d. Reduces electromagnetic interference

24. What is the most likely cause of interference on a network?
    a. Improper cabling and jack choices
    b. Electromagnetic interference from radios and other electrical devices
    c. High voltage device in the vicinity
    d. Problems with the power ground

25. What is the most likely cause of problems with the power ground?
    a. Length of the neutral and ground wires in electrical outlets
    b. Excessive stripping or untwisting of cable
    c. Equipment not located in a climate-controlled area
    d. Poor-quality cabling material used in the network

26. What do long neutral and ground wires in electrical outlets act as?
    a. Lightning rods
    b. Amplifiers for digital signals
    c. Antenna for electrical noise
    d. Line signal dampeners

27. How does electrical noise affect networks?
    a. Shuts down the network
    b. Burns out network devices, especially hubs
    c. Reduces data transmission speed through the network because error-trapping routines are initiated
    d. Distorts or buries digital signals to the point that they become unrecognizable

28. How can the problem of electrical noise be avoided?
    a. By limiting the number and type of electrical devices near the LAN
    b. By working closely with your electrical contractor and the local power company
    c. By making sure all electrical devices are FCC and UL listed
    d. By installing surge suppressors on every network device

29. How can the problem of electrical noise be avoided?
    a. By installing surge suppressors on every network device
    b. By making sure all electrical devices are FCC and UL listed
    c. By getting a single power transformer dedicated to your LAN
    d. By limiting the number and type of electrical devices near the LAN

30. How can having a single power transformer dedicated to your LAN reduce electrical noise?
    a. You can detect and filter out fluctuations in line voltage before it reaches your LAN.
    b. You can specify the size and capacity of the transformer.
    c. You can place the transformer in a central location.
    d. You can control how and where devices such as motors or high current devices are attached.

31. What does installing separate breaker boxes for each office area do to electrical noise?
    a. Reduces chance of electrical noise
    b. Reduces need for surge protectors
    c. Eliminates need for a generator
    d. Eliminates need for network rewiring

Chapter 5   Layer 1: Media, Connections, and Collisions

Introduction

Networking media are the various physical environments through which transmission signals pass. In order for computers to communicate encoded information with each other, networking media must physically connect them to each other. The networking media used to connect computers varies. Several kinds of network media can be used to connect computers:

- Coaxial cable

- Unshielded twisted-pair cable

- Shielded twisted-pair cable

- Fiber-optic cable

Concept Questions

Demonstrate your knowledge of these concepts by answering the following questions in the space provided.

- Networking media is defined as the various physical environments through which transmission signals pass.

- Several types of network media can be used to connect computers. **Identify these different types of network media.**

- Coaxial cable is a type of network media. **Describe how coaxial cable is made.**

- UTP cable is used in a variety of networks. **How many wires make up this type of cable?**

- STP cable combines the techniques of shielding, cancellation, and twisting of wires. **What is shielding and why is it important?**

- Fiber-optic cable is a networking medium. **How does it carry signals?**

- Various criteria, such as rate of data transfer and expense, help determine which type of media should be used. **What media is the fastest and which one is the least expensive?**

- The data link layer of the OSI model provides access to the networking media and physical transmission across the medium. **If you were going to build a network, what media would you use and why?**

Engineering Journal
In the space provided, answer the Concept Questions.

Vocabulary Exercise Chapter 5   **Name:** _____

Date: _____   **Class:** _____

Define the following terms as completely as you can. Use the online Chapter 5 or the *Cisco Systems Networking Academy: First-Year Companion Guide*, Second Edition, material for help.

Bridge

_____

_____

Coaxial cable

_____

_____

Fiber-optic

_____

_____

Hub

_____

_____

Repeater

_____

_____

Router

_____

_____

STP

_____

_____

Switch

_____

_____

Twisted cable

_____

_____

UTP

_____

_____

Focus Questions   **Name:** _____

Date: _____   **Class:** _____

1. Compare and contrast four different Ethernet LAN devices in increasing order of complexity (and typically cost).

_____

_____
_____
_____
_____
_____

2. What are some of the characteristics of shielded twisted pair (STP)?

_____
_____
_____
_____

3. What are some of the characteristics of unshielded twisted pair (UTP)?

_____
_____
_____
_____

4. What are some of the characteristics of coaxial cable?

_____
_____
_____
_____

5. What is the difference between STP and UTP?

_____
_____
_____
_____

6. What is the difference between STP and coaxial cable?

_____
_____
_____
_____

7. What is the advantage of fiber-optic cable?

_____
_____
_____
_____

8. What is the disadvantage of fiber-optic cable?

_____

_____

_____

_____

9. What is the medium for wireless communication?

_____

_____

10. What are EIA/TIA standards?

_____

_____

_____

_____

11. What are patch panels?

_____

_____

12. How many conductors does an RJ45 jack have?

_____

_____

13. What is a shared media environment?

_____

_____

_____

_____

14. Where on a network do collisions occur?

_____

_____

15. What is a collision domain?

_____

_____

16. What happens to the signal in a collision?

_____

_____

17. How do you recognize a collision domain?

_____

_____

18. How do repeaters extend collision domains?

_____

_____

19. How do hubs extend collision domains?

_____

_____

20. Do repeaters filter network traffic?

_____

_____

21. What is the four-repeater rule?

_____

_____

22. How can the segmentation of collision domains be achieved?

_____

_____

23. What is linear bus network topology?

_____

_____

_____

_____

24. What is ring network topology?

_____

_____

25. Are the rings of a dual ring network topology connected?

_____

_____

26. Where is the node of a star network topology located?

_____

_____

27. From a mathematical perspective, where does each node link in an extended star network topology?

_____

_____

28. What is most important when considering the type of networking media to use in an installation?
    a. Management's wishes
    b. Availability of networking media from local sources
    c. Applicable fire, building, and safety codes
    d. Your experience and expertise

29. Which grade of UTP cabling described in the EIA/TIA-568B standard is used for running CDDI and can transmit data at speeds up to 100 Mbps?
    a. Category 2
    b. Category 3
    c. Category 4
    d. Category 5

30. Which grade of UTP cabling described in the EIA/TIA-568B standard is the one most frequently recommended and implemented in installations today?
    a. Category 2
    b. Category 3
    c. Category 4
    d. Category 5

31. What is Category 5 UTP cabling suitable for?
    a. Transmitting data at speeds up to 10 Mbps
    b. Transmitting data at speeds up to 100 Mbps
    c. 10BaseT networks
    d. Token Ring networks

32. What type of STP cable is required by the EIA/TIA-568B standard for horizontal cabling?
    a. Two pair of 100 ohm cable
    b. Two pair of 150 ohm cable
    c. Four pair of 100 ohm cable
    d. Four pair of 150 ohm cable

33. What type of UTP cable is required by the EIA/TIA-568B standard for horizontal cabling?
    a. Two pair of 100 ohm cable
    b. Two pair of 150 ohm cable
    c. Four pair of 100 ohm cable
    d. Four pair of 150 ohm cable

CCNA Exam Review Questions
The following questions help you prepare for the CCNA exam. Answers are found in
Appendix A, "Answers to the CCNA Exam Review Questions."

1. What type of fiber-optic cable is required by the EIA/TIA-568B standard for
    horizontal cabling?
    a. Two pair of 100 ohm cable
    b. Two pair of 150 ohm cable
    c. Two fibers of 62.5/125 um multimode cable
    d. Four fibers of 62.5/125 um multimode cable

2. How can you determine which category of UTP cable any cabling belongs to?
    a. By looking at the end connectors
    b. By reading the UL marking
    c. By measuring the cable diameter
    d. By the color of the cable sheathing

3. Why do networks need to use an access method?
    a. To regulate access to the networking media equitably
    b. To regulate the access of data into certain parts of networking media
    c. To keep unwanted, foreign users from having access to the network
    d. To prioritize data transmissions so that important items have greater access

4. Which of the following best describes an access method?
    a. The method used by software to access network file servers
    b. The method used to verify users as authorized for access to the network
    c. The way users access the network
    d. The way network devices access the network medium

5. Ethernet uses what access method?
    a. Token header transmission protocol
    b. Ethernet does not use an access method
    c. Carrier sense multiple access collision detect
    d. Ethernet transmission carrier collision detect

6. Which of the following best describes a collision?
    a. The frames from two devices impact and are damaged when they meet on the
        physical media.
    b. Two nodes transmit at the same time and one data packet has priority so it
        obliterates the lesser packet.
    c. Two data transmissions cross paths on the network media and corrupt each
        other.
    d. A data transmission is corrupted due to an energy spike over the network
        media.

7. Which of the following best describes a backoff algorithm?
   a. A process wherein the network holds up some data so that other, more important data can get through
   b. The retransmission delay enforced when a collision occurs
   c. The signal that a device on the network sends out to tell the other devices that data is being sent
   d. A mathematical function performed by networking software that prioritizes data packets

Chapter 6   Layer 2: Concepts

Introduction

All data sent out on a network is from a source and is going to a destination. After data is transmitted, the data link layer of the OSI model provides access to the networking media and physical transmission across the media, which enables the data to locate its intended destination on a network. In addition, the data link layer handles error notification, network topology, and flow control. If you refer to the OSI model, you see that the data link layer is adjacent to the physical layer. The data link layer provides reliable transit of data across a physical link. This layer uses Media Access Control (MAC) addresses. In so doing, the data link layer is concerned with physical (as opposed to network, or logical) addressing, network topology, line discipline (how end systems will use the network link), error notification, ordered delivery of frames, and flow control. Moreover, the data link layer uses the MAC address to define a hardware or data link address in order for multiple stations to share the same medium and still uniquely identify each other. Before a data packet is exchanged with a directly connected device on the same LAN, the sending device needs to have a MAC address it can use as a destination address.

Concept Questions

Demonstrate your knowledge of these concepts by answering the following questions in the space provided.

- Every computer, whether it is attached to a network or not, has a unique physical address; no two physical addresses are ever alike. **How is this achieved?**

- The *MAC address*, or the physical address, is located on a *network interface card (NIC)*. Thus, on a network, the NIC is where a device connects to the media.

- Each NIC, which is located in the data link layer of the OSI reference model, has a unique MAC address.

- On a network, when one device wants to send data to another device, it can open a communication pathway to the other device by using the other device's MAC address. **How is this done?**

- When data is sent out on a network by a source, it carries the MAC address of its intended destination. **Does it carry the address of the source?**

- As this data travels along the networking media, the NIC in each device on the network checks whether its MAC address matches the physical destination address carried by the data packet.

Engineering Journal
In the space provided, answer the Concept Questions.

_____
_____
_____
_____
_____
_____
_____
_____
_____
_____
_____
_____
_____
_____
_____
_____
_____
_____
_____
_____
_____
_____
_____
_____
_____
_____
_____
_____
_____
_____
_____
_____
_____
_____
_____
_____
_____
_____
_____
_____
_____
_____
_____
_____
_____

Vocabulary Exercise Chapter 6   Name: _____

Date: _____   **Class:** _____

Define the following terms as completely as you can. Use the online Chapter 6 or the *Cisco Systems Networking Academy: First-Year Companion Guide*, Second Edition, material for help.

Address

_____

_____

Collision domain

_____

_____

CSMA/CD (carrier sense multiple access collision detect)

_____

_____

Data link layer

_____

_____

Encapsulation

_____

_____

Frame

_____

_____

Hexadecimal

_____

_____

IEEE (Institute of Electrical and Electronics Engineers)

_____

_____

LLC (Logical Link Control)

_____

_____

MAC (Media Access Control)

_____

_____

Token Ring

_____

_____

Focus Questions   **Name:** _____

Date: _____   **Class:** _____

1. What are three differences between Layer 1 and Layer 2?

_____

_____

_____

_____

2. Into what sublayers does the IEEE divide the OSI data link layer?

_____

_____

_____

_____

3. What does the LLC do to the network protocol data?

_____

_____

4. Convert the decimal number 24032 to hex.

_____

_____

_____

_____

5. How does a computer identify itself on a network?

_____

_____

_____

_____

6. What is the NIC's role when data is sent out on a network?

_____

_____

_____

_____

_____

_____

_____

_____

7. What is an advantage and a disadvantage to MAC addresses?

_____
_____
_____
_____
_____
_____

8. Which layer does framing belong to?

_____
_____

9. What are the names of the six fields found in a single generic frame?

_____
_____
_____
_____

10. What are the two parts of a package?

_____
_____
_____

11. How does the Frame Check sum help in the delivery of a frame?

_____
_____
_____
_____

12. How does a Token Ring network handle data?

_____
_____
_____

CCNA Exam Review Questions

The following questions help you prepare for the CCNA exam. Answers are found in Appendix A, "Answers to the CCNA Exam Review Questions."

1. Where do all communications on a network originate?
   a. Peripherals
   b. Sources
   c. Computers
   d. Hosts

2. Which of the following best defines a source?
   a. Logically grouped units of information
   b. Network device that receives data
   c. Computer that operates independently from other computers
   d. Network device that is sending data

3. What is a source device?
   a. A source device receives data and information from other computers in a network.
   b. A source device sends data and information to other computers in a network.
   c. A source device is information that moves between computers in a network.
   d. A source device provides connectivity between computers in a network.

4. Where are all communications on a network being sent?
   a. Source
   b. Computer
   c. Data link
   d. Destination

5. Which of the following best defines a destination?
   a. Logically grouped units of information
   b. Network device that is receiving data
   c. Redundant use of equipment to prevent data loss
   d. Network device that is sending data

6. What is another name for link-layer addresses?
   a. IP addresses
   b. Network addresses
   c. Logical addresses
   d. Physical addresses

7. What is another name for link-layer addresses?
   a. MAC addresses
   b. IP addresses
   c. Logical addresses
   d. Network addresses

8. Where are link-layer addresses usually located?
   a. In the routing table
   b. On the NIC
   c. In the ARP cache
   d. In the name server tables

9. On which layer of the OSI model are physical addresses located?
   a. Presentation layer
   b. Session layer
   c. Data link layer
   d. Network layer

10. Which is true about MAC addresses?
    a. Unique for each LAN interface
    b. Located at the network layer
    c. Also called logical addresses
    d. Used to identify host networks

11. Where is the MAC address located?
    a. At the network layer
    b. Burned into ROM at the factory
    c. In the AUI
    d. At the MAU interface

12. Which of the following describes the structure of a MAC address?
    a. 32-bit network identity plus 32-bit host identity
    b. Network, subnet, subnet mask, host
    c. 24-bit vendor code plus 24-bit serial number
    d. Network code plus serial number

13. Which of the following could be a MAC address?
    a. 172.15.5.31
    b. 1111.1111.111
    c. FFFF.FFFF.FFFF
    d. 0000.0c12.3456

14. Which best describes carrier sense multiple access collision detect (CSMA/CD)?
    a. Devices check the channel to make sure no signals are being sent before transmitting data.
    b. Devices transmit data and listen to make sure that they are received properly.
    c. Devices transmit a request prior to transmitting data over the network and wait for an "all clear" reply.
    d. Devices monitor the channel continuously to track and manage traffic.

15. Which of the following is *not* a function of CSMA/CD?
   a.   Transmitting and receiving data packets
   b.   Decoding data packets and checking them for valid addresses
   c.   Detecting errors within data packets or on the network
   d.   Cleaning up collisions on the network medium

Chapter 7   **Layer 2: Technologies**

Introduction

Ethernet was developed by Xerox Corporation's Palo Alto Research Center (PARC) in the 1970s. Ethernet is the most popular LAN standard today. There are millions of devices, or nodes, on Ethernet LANs. The early LANs required very little bandwidth to perform the simple network tasks required at that time—sending/receiving e-mail, transferring data files, and handling print jobs. In 1980, the Institute of Electrical and Electronic Engineers (IEEE) released the IEEE 802.3 specification for which Ethernet was the technological basis. Shortly thereafter, Digital Equipment Corporation, Intel Corporation, and Xerox Corporation jointly developed and released an Ethernet specification (version 2.0) that is substantially compatible with IEEE 802.3. Together, Ethernet and IEEE 802.3 currently maintain the greatest market share of any LAN standard.

An Ethernet LAN transports data between network devices, such as computers, printers, and file servers. Ethernet is known as a shared-medium technology; all the devices are connected to the same delivery media. *Delivery media* refers to the method of transmitting and receiving data. For example, a handwritten letter can be sent (transmitted) using one of many delivery methods, such as the U.S. postal service, Federal Express, or fax. Electronic data can be transmitted via copper cable, thick coaxial cable, thinnet, wireless data transfer, and so on.

Concept Questions

Demonstrate your knowledge of these concepts by answering the following questions in the space provided.

- Ethernet, Fiber Distributed Data Interface (FDDI), and Token Ring are widely used LAN technologies that account for virtually all deployed LANs. LAN standards specify cabling and signaling at the physical and data link layers of the OSI model. Because they are widely adhered to, this book covers the Ethernet and IEEE 802.3 LAN standards. **Why do you suppose that Ethernet technology is so heavily used?**

- When it was developed, Ethernet was designed to fill the middle ground between long-distance, low-speed networks and specialized, computer-room networks carrying data at high speeds for very limited distances. Ethernet is well suited to applications in which a local communication medium must carry sporadic, occasionally heavy traffic at high-peak data rates. **Why is Ethernet so well suited to this kind of traffic?**

- Today, the term *standard Ethernet* refers to all networks using Ethernet (a shared-medium technology) that generally conform to Ethernet specifications, including IEEE 802.3. To use this shared-medium technology, Ethernet uses the carrier sense multiple access collision detection (CSMA/CD) protocol to allow the networking devices to negotiate for the right to transmit. **What are the major benefits of Ethernet?**

Engineering Journal
In the space provided, answer the Concept Questions.

_____
_____
_____
_____
_____
_____
_____
_____
_____
_____
_____
_____
_____
_____
_____
_____
_____
_____
_____
_____
_____
_____
_____
_____
_____
_____
_____
_____
_____
_____
_____
_____
_____
_____
_____
_____
_____
_____
_____

Vocabulary Exercise Chapter 7   Name: _____

Date: _____   Class: _____

Define the following terms as completely as you can. Use the online Chapter 7 or the
Cisco Systems Networking Academy: First-Year Companion Guide, Second Edition,
material for help.

Access control byte

_____
_____
_____

CSMA/CD (carrier sense multiple access collision detect)

_____
_____
_____

Data (Ethernet)

_____
_____
_____

Data (IEEE 802.3)

_____
_____
_____

Destination and source addresses

_____
_____
_____

End delimiter

_____
_____
_____

Ethernet

_____
_____
_____

FDDI

_____
_____
_____

Frame check sequence (FCS)

_____

_____

_____

IEEE 802.3

_____

_____

_____

Length (IEEE 802.3)

_____

_____

_____

Microsegmentation

_____

_____

_____

MSAU

_____

_____

_____

NIC - 1

_____

_____

_____

Preamble

_____

_____

_____

Router

_____

_____

_____

Start delimiter

_____

_____

_____

Focus Questions   **Name:** _____

Date: _____   **Class:** _____

1. What is the size and composition of a token?

_____
_____
_____
_____
_____
_____
_____
_____

2. What does the source address field in an FDDI frame identify?

_____
_____
_____
_____
_____
_____
_____
_____

3. Which field determines whether the frame contains asynchronous or synchronous data?

_____
_____
_____
_____
_____
_____
_____

4. What are two features that are both FDDI and Token Ring share?

_____
_____
_____
_____
_____
_____

5. What are the three advantages that optical fiber has over copper wiring?

_____
_____
_____
_____
_____
_____

6. What network layer device must all network traffic pass through on a star topology?

_____
_____
_____
_____
_____
_____

7. What is the purpose of a NIC?

_____
_____
_____
_____
_____
_____

8. What are two reasons why LANs are segmented?

_____
_____
_____
_____
_____
_____

9. Ethernet uses which access method to detect errors within data packets or on the network?

_____
_____
_____
_____
_____
_____

10. Why is it cost efficient to have a switched LAN environment?

_____
_____
_____

CCNA Exam Review Questions
The following questions help prepare you for the CCNA Exam. Answers are found in
Appendix A, "Answers to the CCNA Exam Review Questions."

1. Which best describes the data link layer of the OSI model?
   a. Transmits data to other network layers
   b. Provides services to application processes
   c. Takes weak signals, cleans them, amplifies them, and sends them on their way across the network
   d. Provides reliable transit of data across a physical link

2. Which layer provides reliable transit of data across a physical link?
   a. Data link
   b. Physical
   c. Application
   d. Transport

3. What processes is the data link layer concerned with?
   a. Physical addressing, network topology, line discipline, error notification, ordered delivery of frames, and flow control
   b. Establishing, managing, and terminating sessions between applications and managing data exchange between presentation layer entities
   c. Synchronizing cooperating applications and establishing agreement on procedures for error recovery and control of data integrity
   d. Providing mechanisms for the establishment, maintenance, and termination of virtual circuits, transport fault detection, recovery, and information flow control

4. Physical addressing and network topology are handled by which layer?
   a. Physical
   b. Presentation
   c. Data link
   d. Session

5. On a network, where does a device connect to the media?
   a. Ethernet card
   b. Hub
   c. Router
   d. NIC card

6. What is another name for the MAC address?
   a. Binary address
   b. Octadecimal address
   c. Physical address
   d. TCP/IP address

7. In which layer is the MAC address located?
    a. Session
    b. Data link
    c. Physical
    d. Transport

8. What does MAC address stand for?
    a. Macintosh Access Capable
    b. Mainframe Advisory Council
    c. Media Access Control
    d. Machine Application Communication

9. Which of the following items is located in the data link layer?
    a. Destination
    b. Peripheral
    c. Repeater
    d. MAC address

10. What is required for every port or device that connects to a network?
    a. Repeater
    b. Termination
    c. MAC or physical address
    d. ATM switch

11. Which of the following best describes MAC addressing?
    a. Addresses reside in the NIC card and are assigned by their manufacturers.
    b. Addresses are assigned by the IEEE committee and need to be requested by the network administrator.
    c. Addresses are determined by the distance of the computer from the network hub.
    d. Addresses are given to every computer when they are manufactured.

12. How does a source device locate the destination for data on a network?
    a. The NIC at the destination identifies its MAC address in a data packet.
    b. A data packet stops at the destination.
    c. The NIC at the destination sends its MAC address to the source.
    d. The source sends a unique data packet to each MAC address on the network.

13. Which of the following best describes internetworking devices?
    a. Products that determine the optimal path along which network traffic should be forwarded
    b. Products that contain multiple independent, connected modules of network equipment
    c. Network connections or a junction common to two or more lines in a network
    d. Products used to connect separate networks to each other

Chapter 8   Design and Documentation

Introduction

Of all the organizations mentioned here, the EIA/TIA has had the greatest impact on networking media standards. The EIA/TIA standards were developed with the intent of identifying minimum requirements that would support multiproduct and multivendor environments. Moreover, these standards were developed so that they allow for planning and installation of LAN systems without knowledge of the specific equipment that is to be installed. Thus, the EIA/TIA standards allow the LAN designer options and room for expansion. Specifically, the EIA/TIA-568B standards for technical performance of the networking media have been, and continue to be, the most widely used. The EIA/TIA standards address six elements of cabling for LAN systems: horizontal cabling, telecommunications closets, backbone cabling, equipment rooms, work areas, and entrance facilities.

EIA/TIA-568B defines *horizontal cabling* as a networking medium that runs from the telecommunications outlet to the horizontal cross-connect. This element includes the networking medium that is run along a horizontal pathway, the telecommunications outlet or connector, the mechanical terminations in the wiring closet, and the patch cords or jumpers in the wiring closet. In short, horizontal cabling describes the networking medium that is used in the area extending from the wiring closet to a workstation.

After you successfully run cable in a horizontal cabling run, connections must be made in the wiring closet. A *wiring closet* is a specially designed room used for wiring a data or voice network. Because a wiring closet serves as a central junction point for the wiring and wiring equipment that is used for connecting devices in a LAN, it is at the center point of a star topology. Typically, the equipment found in a wiring closet can include patch panels, wiring hubs, bridges, switches, and routers.

Generally, the wiring closet must be large enough to accommodate the equipment and wiring located in it. Naturally, this varies with the size of the LAN and the types of equipment required to operate it. Equipment required for some small LANs might take up as little space as a large filing cabinet, whereas a large LAN could require a full-fledged computer room. Finally, the wiring closet must be large enough to accommodate future growth.

Concept Questions

Demonstrate your knowledge of these concepts by answering the following questions in the space provided.

- EIA/TIA standards govern the type of networking media that can be used in the horizontal cabling of LANs. **What type of networking media can be used with horizontal cabling?**
- Any time you install cable, it is important to document what you have done. **How would you document the kind of cable used in a network?**

- A wiring closet is a specially designed room used for wiring a data or voice network. **What attributes are necessary for a working wiring closet?**

- The IEEE and the EIA/TIA have established standards that allow you to evaluate whether your network is operating at an acceptable level after installation has been completed. **What are some of those standards?**

- Cable testers can perform tests that measure the overall capability of a cable run. Cable testers use a feature called wire map to indicate which wire pairs connect to what pins on lugs and sockets. **Describe how you would use a cable tester to measure the capability of the cable run.**

- If not properly addressed, AC power line noise can present problems for a network. **Why does the noise cause problems for the network?**

- The problem of sags and brownouts can best be addressed through the use of UPSs.

Engineering Journal
In the space provided, answer the Concept Questions.

_____
_____
_____
_____
_____
_____
_____
_____
_____
_____
_____
_____
_____
_____
_____
_____
_____
_____
_____
_____
_____
_____
_____
_____

Vocabulary Exercise Chapter 8   **Name:** _____

Date: _____   **Class:** _____

Define the following terms as completely as you can. Use the online Chapter 8 or the
Cisco Systems Networking Academy: First-Year Companion Guide, Second Edition,
material for help.

Backbone

_____
_____
_____

Catchment areas

_____
_____
_____

HCC

_____
_____
_____

Hierarchical star

_____
_____
_____

Hub

_____
_____
_____

IDF

_____
_____
_____

MCC

_____
_____
_____

MDF

_____

_____

_____

Micron

_____

_____

_____

Oscillation

_____

_____

_____

Patch panel

_____

_____

_____

PBX

_____

_____

_____

POP

_____

_____

_____

Sag

_____

_____

_____

Spike

_____

_____

_____

Surge

_____

_____

_____

Focus Questions   **Name:** _____

Date: _____   **Class:** _____

1. Where is the patch panel and hub located in a star topology?

_____
_____
_____
_____
_____
_____

2. How much weight per square meter must the floor of the MDF be able to bear?

_____
_____
_____

3. What problem could result if the humidity level in the MDF is above 50 percent?

_____
_____
_____
_____
_____
_____

4. Why should fluorescent lighting be avoided in a wiring closet?

_____
_____
_____
_____
_____
_____

5. What types of devices might be connected to a network?

_____
_____
_____
_____
_____
_____

6. What is the difference between and MDF and an IDF?

_____
_____
_____

7. Is one wiring closet adequate for a multibuilding campus?

_____
_____
_____

8. What is the difference between and normal mode problem and a common mode problem?

_____
_____
_____
_____
_____
_____

9. Why is a common mode problem more serious than a normal mode problem?

_____
_____
_____
_____
_____

10. What is a surge?

_____
_____
_____
_____
_____

11. What is a sag?

_____
_____
_____
_____
_____

12. What is a spike?

_____
_____
_____
_____
_____

CCNA Exam Review Questions

The following questions help you pass the CCNA exam. Answers are found in Appendix A, "Answers to the CCNA Exam Review Questions."

1. Which of the following does *not* describe a wiring closet?
    a. Room used for housing the wiring for a voice network
    b. Room used for housing the wiring for a data network
    c. Room at the center of a Token Ring topology
    d. Room at the center point of a star topology

2. Which of the following equipment is *not* typically found in a wiring closet?
    a. Telecommunications outlets
    b. Patch panels
    c. Wiring hubs
    d. Routers

3. What is a wiring closet?
    a. Room where electrical power enters a commercial building
    b. Room used for housing the wiring for a data or voice network
    c. Room at the center of a token ring network
    d. Room where the entire power supply to a commercial building can be controlled

4. In a large network, what is a wiring closet that other wiring closets are dependent upon called?
    a. Master wiring facility (MWF)
    b. Master star topology (MST)
    c. Main distribution facility (MDF)
    d. Extended star topology (EST)

5. What is the difference between a main distribution facility (MDF) and intermediate distribution facility (IDF)?
    a. The MDF contains the primary network server and the major network devices while the IDFs contain only the necessary additional routers and repeaters.
    b. The MDF is on the lowest floor in a multifloor network while the IDFs are on upper floors.
    c. The MDF has all the bridges, hubs, routers, and ports needed for the network while the IDFs hold any needed repeaters.
    d. The MDF is the primary communications room and the central point in the network while the IDFs are secondary communications rooms dependent upon the MDF.

6. Which of the following is *not* a feature of a network with more than one wiring closet?
    a. Dependent star topologies
    b. An MDF
    c. An IDF
    d. An extended star topology

7. What type of network topology usually has more than one wiring closet?
    a. Token Ring
    b. Extended star
    c. Tree
    d. Bus

8. Which of the following best describes a type of connection made at the LAN patch panel?
    a. Network device ports connect directly to patch panel pins.
    b. Horizontal cabling runs connect directly to the horizontal cross-connect.
    c. Horizontal cabling runs connect directly to telecommunications outlets.
    d. Patch cords connect the horizontal cross-connect directly to the patch panel.

9. Which of the following is *not* a type of connection made at the LAN patch panel?
    a. Patch cords interconnect computers and hubs.
    b. Patch cords directly connect devices to telecommunications ports.
    c. Horizontal cabling runs are terminated at the patch panel.
    d. Patch cords connect the horizontal cross-connect directly to the patch panel.

Chapter 9   Structured Cabling

Introduction

After the decision is made to network computers in a building, one of the first things you must address is where the wiring closet will be located. To determine where the wiring closet will be located, it will help to think of the hub as the center point of a circle with lines of horizontal cabling radiating out from it like spokes from the center of a wheel. Then, locate all the devices that will be connected to the network on a floor plan of the building that is drawn approximately to scale. As you do this, remember that computers will not be the only devices you will want to connect to the network. You must also consider the location of printers and file servers that will be part of the network.

When you connect cable to jacks, remember to strip back only as much of the cable's jacket as is required to terminate the wires. The more wire that is exposed, the poorer the connection is. This results in signal loss. In addition, maintain the twists in each pair of wires as close as possible to the point of termination. It is the twisting of the wires that produces cancellation, which is needed to prevent radio and electromagnetic interference. For Category 4 UTP, the maximum amount of untwisting that is allowed is 1 inch. For Category 5 UTP, the maximum amount of untwisting that is allowed is ½ inch.

If multiple cables are run over the same path, use cable ties to cinch them together. When cable ties are needed to mount or secure cable, be sure to apply cable ties so they can slide a little. Position ties at random intervals along the cable. Never secure the cable ties too tightly; this can damage the cable. When securing the cable ties, try to minimize the amount of jacket twisting. If cable is twisted too much, it can lead to torn cable jackets.

Never allow the cable to be pinched or kinked. If this occurs, data moves more slowly and your LAN operates at less than optimal capacity.

When handling the cable, avoid stretching it. If you exceed 25 pounds of pull, wires inside the cable can untwist. As you have learned, if wire pairs become untwisted, this can lead to interference and crosstalk. Above all, never cut corners with cable. It is important to leave ample slack. Remember, a few feet of extra cable is a small price to pay to avoid having to redo a cable run because of mistakes resulting in stretched cable. Most cable installers avoid this problem by leaving enough slack so that the cable can reach the floor and extend another two or three feet at both ends of the cable. Other installers follow the practice of leaving a *service coil*, which is nothing more than a few extra feet of cable left coiled up inside the ceiling or in another out-of-the-way location.

Use appropriate and recommended techniques for dressing and securing the cable. These include cable ties, cable support bars, wire management panels, and releasable Velcro straps. Never use a staple gun to position cables. Staples can pierce the jacket, which results in loss of connection.

Concept Questions

Demonstrate your knowledge of these concepts by answering the following questions in the space provided.

- Generally speaking, the wiring closet must be large enough to accommodate the equipment and wiring located in it. **How do you determine how large the closet should be?**

  - Naturally, this varies with the size of the LAN and the types of equipment required to operate it. Equipment required for some small LANs might take up as little space as a large filing cabinet, while a large LAN could require a full-fledged computer room.

- Finally, the wiring closet must be large enough to accommodate future growth. **How do you estimate the future growth of a network?**

  - EIA/TIA-569 specifies that there be a minimum of one wiring closet per floor and states that additional wiring closets should be provided for each area up to 1000 square meters when the floor area served exceeds 1000 square meters or the horizontal cabling distance exceeds 90 meters. *Hint:* 1000 square meters equals 10,000 square feet. Ninety meters equals approximately 300 feet.

- Anytime you install cable, it is important to document what you have done. Therefore, as you install cable, be sure to make a *cut sheet*. A cut sheet is a rough diagram that shows where cable runs are. It also indicates what the numbers of the schoolrooms, offices, or other rooms are where the cable runs lead to. **Draw and document the cabling for a small LAN. Include three terminals in three different rooms and provide for Internet access.**

  - Later, you can refer to this cut sheet so that corresponding numbers can be placed on all telecommunications outlets and at the patch panel in the wiring closet. You can use a page in your journal to document cable runs. By placing it in your journal, you have an additional layer of documentation for any cable installation.

- EIA/TIA-606 specifies that some kind of unique identifier must be given to each hardware termination unit. This identifier must be marked on each termination hardware unit or on its label. When identifiers are used at the work area, station terminations must be labeled on the faceplate housing, or on the connector itself. Whether they are adhesive or insertable, all labels must meet legibility, defacement and adhesion requirements. **Label the drawing that you did earlier in this exercise with the identifier to each hardware termination unit.**

Engineering Journal
In the space provided, answer the Concept Questions.

Vocabulary Exercise Chapter 9   **Name:** _____

Date: _____   **Class:** _____

Define the following terms as completely as you can. Use the online Chapter 9 or the
Cisco Systems Networking Academy: First-Year Companion Guide, Second Edition,
material for help.

Algorithm

_____
_____
_____

Backbone

_____
_____
_____

Backoff

_____
_____
_____

Bus

_____
_____
_____

Bus topology

_____
_____
_____

Catchment

_____
_____
_____

Collision

_____
_____
_____

Collision domain

_____
_____
_____

Cut sheet

_____
_____
_____

EIA-TIA-606

_____
_____
_____

Fish tape

_____
_____
_____

Gutter

_____
_____
_____

Hammer drill

_____
_____
_____

HCC

_____
_____
_____

Hierarchical star topology

_____
_____
_____

Highway

_____
_____
_____

ICC

_____
_____
_____

IDF

_____
_____
_____

MCC

_____
_____
_____

MDF

_____
_____
_____

Noise

_____
_____
_____

Patch panels

_____
_____
_____

Pin locations

_____
_____
_____

POP

_____
_____
_____

Ports

_____
_____
_____

Pull string

_____

_____

_____

Punch-down tool

_____

_____

_____

Raceway

_____

_____

_____

RJ connector

_____

_____

_____

Signal injector

_____

_____

_____

Star topology

_____

_____

_____

Telepole

_____

_____

_____

Tie Wraps

_____

_____

_____

Wire maps

_____

_____

_____

Focus Questions   **Name:** _____

Date: _____   **Class:** _____

1. Where are patch cables plugged into?

_____
_____
_____

2. Think about the cabling in this building. What factors would the person laying cable have to keep in mind? How would they keep track of all the cables?

_____
_____
_____
_____
_____
_____

3. How do you determine whether cable has been properly installed?

_____
_____
_____

4. What do you call an assembly of pin locations and ports that can be mounted on a rack?

_____
_____
_____
_____
_____
_____

5. What type of vertical cabling connects the central hub to other hubs in a hierarchical star topology?

_____
_____
_____

6. What type of tool is used to measure attenuation of a signal on a network?

_____
_____
_____
_____
_____
_____

CCNA Exam Review Questions

The following questions help you prepare for the CCNA Exam. Answers are found in Appendix A, "Answers to the CCNA Exam Review Questions."

1. Which of the following statements best describes the EIA/TIA-569 specification for wiring closets?
    a. There should be a minimum of one wiring closet for every floor of a building.
    b. There should be a maximum of one wiring closet for every floor of a building.
    c. There should be a minimum of two wiring closets for every floor of a building.
    d. There should be a maximum of two wiring closets for every floor of a building.

2. Which of the following best describes the EIA/TIA-569 standard for additional wiring closets?
    a. Additional wiring closets should be provided for each area up to 90 square meters when the floor area served exceeds 90 square meters or the horizontal cabling distance exceeds 90 meters.
    b. Additional wiring closets should be provided for each area up to 100 square meters when the floor area served exceeds 100 square meters or the horizontal cabling distance exceeds 9 meters.
    c. Additional wiring closets should be provided for each area up to 1000 square meters when the floor area served exceeds 1000 square meters or the horizontal cabling distance exceeds 30 meters.
    d. Additional wiring closets should be provided for each area up to 1000 square meters when the floor area served exceeds 1000 square meters or the horizontal cabling distance exceeds 90 meters.

3. If Acme Inc., occupies 3500 square meters on the second floor of a building, how many wiring closets should be installed according to EIA/TIA 569?
    a. One
    b. Two
    c. Three
    d. Four

4. If Acme Inc., occupies the first three floors of a building and each floor is 1500 square meters, how many wiring closets should be installed according to EIA/TIA 569?
    a. One
    b. Three
    c. Six
    d. Nine

5. Which of the following is *not* a specification for walls, floors, and ceilings of a wiring closet?
   a. A minimum of 15 feet of wall space should be provided for terminations and related equipment for the POP.
   b. Rooms selected for wiring closets should have a dropped or false ceiling for easy access.
   c. Interior walls on which equipment is to be mounted should be covered with ¾" plywood that is raised away from the underlying wall a minimum of 1 ¾".
   d. Floor coverings should be tile or other type of finished surface to help control dust.

6. What is a Point of Presence (POP)?
   a. The point where the horizontal cabling connects to the backbone
   b. The point where the electrical power lines enter the building
   c. The point where the telephone company's equipment and the building's main distribution facility connect
   d. The point where the network and the electrical system of the building connect

7. Why should wiring closets *not* have a dropped or false ceiling?
   a. The minimum ceiling height specified by EIA/TIA-569 cannot be met in most rooms with most dropped or false ceilings.
   b. The temperature and humidity cannot be adequately controlled.
   c. Dust from the ceiling materials poses a problem for long term equipment maintenance.
   d. Access is not controlled because people can get into the room through the ceiling.

8. What kind of floor should the wiring room have?
   a. Tile or other finished surface
   b. Carpet
   c. Unfinished stone
   d. Electronics grade carpet

9. What is the minimum and maximum relative humidity level that should be maintained for rooms serving as wiring closets?
   a. Between 10% and 50%
   b. Between 20% and 70%
   c. Between 30% and 50%
   d. Between 30% and 70%

10. What should the approximate temperature in a wiring closet be when all LAN equipment is fully functioning?
    a. 60 degrees Fahrenheit
    b. 65 degrees Fahrenheit
    c. 70 degrees Fahrenheit
    d. 75 degrees Fahrenheit

11. Which of the following is *not* a requirement for lighting fixtures or power outlets in a wiring closet?
    a. Fluorescent lighting is recommended to avoid outside interference.
    b. A wall switch to turn room lighting on and off should be located immediately inside the door.
    c. At least one duplex power outlet should be located every ten feet along each wall in a main distribution facility.
    d. At least two duplex power outlets should be located along each wall if the wiring closet is to serve as an intermediate distribution facility.

12. Why should fluorescent light fixtures be avoided in wiring closets?
    a. They provide false color lighting, which can lead to mistakes in making connections.
    b. They generate outside electrical interference.
    c. They can degrade some plastic materials used in network equipment.
    d. There often is insufficient room in a wiring closet to change out the fluorescent bulbs easily and safely.

13. Which of the following is *not* a requirement for room and equipment access in a wiring closet?
    a. The door should be at least three feet wide and should swing open out of the room to ensure easy access to the room for workers and equipment.
    b. The wiring closet should lock from an outside access in such a way that exiting from the room is always possible.
    c. Wiring hubs and patch panels may be wall-mounted using hinged wall brackets that are attached to the plywood covering the underlying wall surface.
    d. When a distribution rack is used to mount patch panels and wiring hubs, the minimum distance for the rack from the wall should be six inches.

14. Which of the following is *not* a wiring closet specification for cable access and support?
    a. Access to the wiring closet for all horizontal cabling coming from the work areas should be via a raised floor.
    b. All cable leaving the room to intermediate distribution facilities and computer and communications rooms located on other floors of a building should be via four-inch conduits or sleeved cores.
    c. One excess sleeved core or conduit should be provided in each wiring closet in order to provide for future anticipated growth.
    d. Any wall or ceiling openings provided for conduits or sleeved cores must be sealed with smoke and flame retardant materials.

15. What is the first step in locating a wiring closet for a network?
    a. Identify the number of computers that will be part of the network.
    b. Identify the number of printers and file servers that will be part of the network.

    c. Identify all devices that will be connected to the network on a floor plan.

    d. Identify the topological requirements of devices that will be in the network.

16. Which of the following would *not* be considered when selecting a potential location for a wiring closet?

    a. Identify a secure location close to the POP.

    b. Determine the exact number of wiring closets needed for the network.

    c. Determine the location of the building's communication facilities.

    d. Make an initial selection of potential locations based on EIA/TIA-569 specifications.

17. What is the name for the most centrally located wiring closet in a LAN with an extended star typology?

    a. Catchment area

    b. Main distribution facility

    c. Intermediate distribution facility

    d. Repeated distribution facility

18. Where should the main distribution facility (MDF) be located if a LAN with an extended star topology is used in a multistory building?

    a. Next to the POP

    b. On the first floor

    c. On one of the middle floors

    d. In the basement

19. Where should a repeater be located in a LAN with an extended star topology?

    a. Catchment area

    b. Main distribution facility

    c. Intermediate distribution facility

    d. Repeated distribution facility

20. What network device is used in an extended star topology when the catchment area of one wiring closet is not enough?

    a. Repeater

    b. Backoff

    c. Terminator

    d. Suppressor

21. What type of cabling provides interconnections between wiring closets, wiring closets and the POP, and between buildings that are part of the same LAN?

    a. Token Ring cabling

    b. Backbone cabling

    c. Coaxial cabling

    d. Horizontal cabling

22. What type of cabling is used to connect the POP to the MDF when an Ethernet LAN is in a multistory building?
    a. Backbone cabling
    b. Coaxial cabling
    c. Horizontal cabling
    d. Token Ring cabling

23. What type of cabling is used to connect an MDF to IDFs when an Ethernet LAN is in a multistory building?
    a. Token Ring cabling
    b. Backbone cabling
    c. Coaxial cabling
    d. Horizontal cabling

24. What type of cabling is used to connect IDFs on each floor to the various work areas when an Ethernet LAN is in a multistory building?
    a. Backbone cabling
    b. Coaxial cabling
    c. Horizontal cabling
    d. Token Ring cabling

25. Which type of networking media is installed most often for backbone cabling?
    a. 100 ohm unshielded twisted pair cable
    b. 150 ohm shielded twisted pair cable
    c. 62.5/125 micron optical fiber cable
    d. 50 ohm coaxial cable

26. Which of the following types of networking media is not recommended for backbone cabling?
    a. 100 ohm unshielded twisted-pair cable
    b. 150 ohm shielded twisted-pair cable
    c. 62.5/125-micron optical-fiber cable
    d. 50 ohm coaxial cable

27. What kind of connection is used in a wiring closet where the horizontal cabling connects to a patch panel that is connected by backbone cabling to the main distribution facility?
    a. Horizontal cross-connect
    b. Vertical cross-connect
    c. Intermediate cross-connect
    d. Main cross-connect

28. What kind of connection is used in a wiring closet that serves as the most central point in a star topology and where LAN backbone cabling connects to the Internet?
    a. Horizontal cross-connect
    b. Vertical cross-connect

    c. Intermediate cross-connect
    d. Main cross-connect

29. What kind of connection is used in an IDF that connects the horizontal cross-connect to the main cross-connect?
    a. Horizontal cross-connect
    b. Vertical cross-connect
    c. Intermediate cross-connect
    d. Main cross-connect

30. What is the maximum distance for backbone cabling if single-mode, fiber-optic cable is used to connect the horizontal cross-connect to the main cross-connect?
    a. 500 meters
    b. 1000 meters
    c. 2500 meters
    d. 3000 meters

31. What is the maximum distance for backbone cabling if single-mode, fiber-optic cable is used to connect the intermediate cross-connect to the main cross-connect?
    a. 500 meters
    b. 1000 meters
    c. 2500 meters
    d. 3000 meters

32. What is the maximum distance for backbone cabling if single-mode, fiber-optic cable is used to connect the horizontal cross-connect to the intermediate cross-connect?
    a. 500 meters
    b. 1000 meters
    c. 2500 meters
    d. 3000 meters

Chapter 10   Layer 3: Routing and Addressing

Introduction

The network layer interfaces to networks and provides the best end-to-end packet delivery services to its user, the transport layer. The network layer sends packets from the source network to the destination network.

Routers are devices that implement the network service. They provide interfaces for a wide range of links and subnetworks at a wide range of speeds. Routers are active and intelligent network nodes and thus can participate in managing the network. Routers manage networks by providing dynamic control over resources and supporting the tasks and goals for networks: connectivity, reliable performance, management control, and flexibility.

In addition to the basic switching and routing functions, routers have implemented a variety of value-added features that help to improve the cost-effectiveness of the network. These features include sequencing traffic based on priority and traffic filtering.

Typically, routers are required to support multiple protocol stacks, each with its own routing protocols, and to allow these different environments to operate in parallel. In practice, routers also incorporate bridging functions and can serve as a limited form of hub.

IP addressing makes it possible for data passing over the network media of the Internet to find its destination. Because each IP address is a 32-bit value, there are four billion different IP address possibilities. IP addresses are hierarchical addresses, like phone numbers and zip codes. They provide a better way to organize computer addresses than MAC addresses, which are flat addresses (like social security numbers). IP addresses can be set in software and are thus flexible. MAC addresses are burned into hardware. Both addressing schemes are important for efficient communications between computers.

Concept Questions

Demonstrate your knowledge of these concepts by answering the following questions in the space provided.

Path determination occurs at the network layer. Routers are another type of internetworking device. These devices pass data packets between networks based on network protocol or Layer 3 information. **Explain how this process works.**

Routers have the ability to make intelligent decisions as to the best path for delivery of data on the network. **What criteria do they use to make these decisions?**

IP addresses are 32-bit values written as four octets separated with periods. To make them easier to remember, IP addresses are usually written in dotted notation using decimal numbers. IP addresses are used to identify a machine on a network and thenetwork to which it is attached. **What do each of the numbers mean?**

Hexadecimal is a Base 16 numbering system that is used to represent MAC addresses. It is referred to as Base 16 because it uses 16 symbols; combinations of these symbols can then represent all possible numbers. Because only 10 symbols represent digits (0, 1, 2, 3, 4, 5, 6, 7, 8, 9), and Base 16 requires 6 more symbols, the extra symbols are the letters A, B, C, D, E, and F.

The position of each symbol, or digit, in a hex number represents the base number 16 raised to a power, or exponent, based on its position. Moving from right to left, the first position represents 16^0, or 1; the second position represents 16^1, or 16; the third position, 16^2, or 256; and so on.

Example:
1 2 3 4 5 6 7 8 9 10 11 12 13 14 15 16
0 1 2 3 4 5 6 7 8 9 A B C D E F

$4F6A = (4 \times 16^3) + (F[15] \times 16^2) + (6 \times 16^1) + (A[10] \times 16^0)$

Convert Decimal to Hex
Converting from decimal to binary is done with a procedure called the *remainder method*. This method uses successive divisions of the base number of the system. You can use the same method to convert decimal into hex, or Base 16.

Example:
24,032 / 16 = 16 into 24,032 is 1502, with a remainder of 0
1502 / 16 = 16 into 1502 is 93, with a remainder of 14, or E
93 / 16 = 16 into 93 is 5, with a remainder of 13, or D
13 / 16 = 16 into 13 is 0, with a remainder of 3

By collecting all the remainders backward, we have the hex number 3DE0.

Convert These Decimal Numbers to Binary:
32,014   Hex number =
56,432   Hex number =
57,845   Hex number =
98,764   Hex number =
54,462   Hex number =

Convert Hex to Decimal

Convert hexadecimal numbers to decimal numbers by multiplying the hex digits by the base number of the system, in this case, Base 16, raised to the exponent of the position.

Example:

Convert the hex number 3F4B to decimal (Work from right to left.)

$$
\begin{aligned}
B \times 16^3 &= 12{,}288 \\
F(15) \times 16^2 &= 3840 \\
4 \times 16^1 &= 64 \\
B(11) \times 16^0 &= 11 \\
\hline
16{,}203 &= \text{decimal equivalent}
\end{aligned}
$$

Convert These Hex Numbers to Decimal:

23F6   Decimal =

6AB7   Decimal =

5FE3   Decimal =

87CE   Decimal =

59AC   Decimal =

Engineering Journal

In the space provided, answer the Concept Questions.

_____

_____

_____

_____

_____

_____

_____

_____

_____

_____

_____

_____

_____

_____

_____

_____

_____

_____

_____

_____

_____

Engineering Journal (Continued)

Vocabulary Exercise Chapter 10   Name: _____

Date: _____   Class: _____

Define the following terms as completely as you can. Use the online Chapter 10 or the *Cisco Systems Networking Academy: First-Year Companion Guide*, Second Edition, material for help.

Segment

_____
_____
_____

Internet service providers (ISPs)

_____
_____
_____

Router

_____
_____
_____

Address

_____
_____
_____

IP

_____
_____
_____

Broadcast address

_____
_____
_____

Subnetwork

_____
_____
_____

Subnet mask

_____

_____

_____

Focus Questions   **Name:** _____

Date: _____   **Class:** _____

1. What type of addressing scheme does the network layer address use?

    _____

    _____

    _____

2. The Internet is a collection of network _____ that are tied together to facilitate
    the sharing of information.

    _____

    _____

    _____

3. What specific internetworking device that operates at Layer 3 interconnects
    networks?

    _____

    _____

    _____

4. What type of determination is the process the router uses to choose a course for the
    packet to travel to its destination?

    _____

    _____

    _____

5. At what layer does addressing occur?

    _____

    _____

    _____

6. When a computer is moved to a different network, what type of address remains the
    same and what type of address must be reassigned?

    _____

    _____

    _____

7. What is the difference between a flat addressing scheme and a hierarchical addressing
    scheme?

    _____

    _____

    _____

8. In the IP header, what information does the "total length" contain?

_____

_____

_____

9. What three pieces of information does the subnet mask give to network devices?

_____

_____

_____

10. How many hosts can be assigned to a Class C network?

_____

_____

_____

CCNA Exam Review Questions
The following questions help you review for the CCNA exam. Answers are found in Appendix A, "Answers to the CCNA Exam Review Questions."

1. Which layer of the OSI model uses the Internet Protocol addressing scheme to determine the best way to move data from one place to another?
   a. Physical layer
   b. Data link layer
   c. Network layer
   d. Transport layer

2. What function allows routers to evaluate available routes to a destination and to establish the preferred handling of a packet?
   a. Data linkage
   b. Path determination
   c. SDLC interface protocol
   d. Frame Relay

3. IP addresses are necessary for which of the following reasons?
   a. To identify a machine on a network and the network to which it is attached
   b. To identify a machine on a network
   c. To identify the network
   d. To keep track of whom is on a network

4. Which of the following best describes a network address on the Internet?
   a. All four octets in the address are different.
   b. Each address is unique.
   c. The first three octets can be the same, but the last one must be different.
   d. Two of the four octets can be the same, but the other two have to be different.

5. Who assigns the network portion of every IP address?
   a. The local network administrator
   b. The person who owns the computer
   c. The Network Information Center
   d. The host network administrator

6. The network number plays what part in an IP address?
   a. Specifies the network to which the host belongs
   b. Specifies the identity of the computer on the network
   c. Specifies which node on the subnetwork is being addressed
   d. Specifies which networks the device can communicate with

7. The host number plays what part in an IP address?
   a. Designates the identity of the computer on the network
   b. Designates which node on the subnetwork is being addressed
   c. Designates the network to which the host belongs
   d. Designates which hosts the device can communicate with

8. A Class A address is given to what sort of organization?
   a. An individual
   b. A medium-size company
   c. A large corporation
   d. A government

9. In a Class A address, how many of the octets are assigned by InterNIC?
   a. The first octet is assigned by NIC.
   b. The first and second octet are assigned by NIC.
   c. The first, second, and third octets are assigned by NIC.
   d. All the octets are assigned by InterNIC.

10. In a Class A address, the value of the first octet can equal which of the following?
    a. The value of first octet is 0 through 127.
    b. The value of first octet is 128 through 191.
    c. The value of first octet is 192 through 223.
    d. The value of first octet is 192 through 255.

11. A Class B address is given to what sort of organization?
    a. An individual
    b. A medium-size company
    c. A large corporation
    d. A government

12. In a Class B address, how many of the octets are assigned locally?
    a. The first octet is assigned locally.
    b. The second octet is assigned locally.
    c. The second and third octets are assigned locally.
    d. The third and fourth octets are assigned locally.

13. The following address is of which class? 129.21.89.76
    a. A Class A address.
    b. A Class B address.
    c. A Class C address.
    d. This address could not be used.

14. A Class C address is given to what sort of organization?
    a. An individual
    b. A medium-size company
    c. A huge corporation
    d. A government

15. Which of the following addresses is a Class C address?
    a. 129.219.95.193
    b. 209.101.218.30
    c. 151.13.27.38
    d. 192.119.15.17

Engineering Journal (Continued)

Chapter 11   Layer 3: Protocols

Introduction
Protocols determine whether data is passed beyond the network layer to higher levels of the OSI model. Basically, for this to occur, the data packet must contain both a destination MAC address and a destination IP address. If it lacks one or the other, the data does not pass to the upper levels. In this way, MAC addresses and IP addresses act as a sort of "check and balance" for each other.

Concept Questions

Demonstrate your knowledge of these concepts by answering the following questions in the space provided.

- If the destination is to retain the data and pass it along to the upper layers of the OSI model, the source must use both a destination MAC address and a destination IP address. Therefore, the device initiates a process called an Address Resolution Protocol (ARP) request that is designed to help it discover what the destination MAC address is. **How does the device know to initiate the ARP request?**

- The protocol that a device uses when it does not know its own IP address is the Reverse Address Resolution Protocol (RARP). Like ARP, RARP binds MAC addresses to IP addresses so that network devices can use them to encapsulate data before sending it out on the network. **Can you explain how this works?**

Engineering Journal
In the space provided, answer the Concept Questions.

_____
_____
_____
_____
_____
_____
_____
_____
_____
_____
_____
_____
_____
_____
_____
_____
_____
_____

Engineering Journal (Continued)

Vocabulary Exercise Chapter 11 Name: _____

Date: _____ Class: _____

Define the following terms as completely as you can. Use the online Chapter 11 or the *Cisco Systems Networking Academy: First-Year Companion Guide*, Second Edition, material for help.

ARP (Address Resolution Protocol)

_____
_____
_____

BOOTP

_____
_____
_____

Connection oriented

_____
_____
_____

Connectionless

_____
_____
_____

Datagram routing

_____
_____
_____

Dynamic address resolution

_____
_____
_____

Enhanced IGRP (Enhanced Interior Gateway Routing Protocol)

_____
_____
_____

ICMP (Internet Control Message Protocol)

_____
_____
_____

IP (Internet Protocol)

_____
_____
_____

IP address

_____
_____
_____

RARP (Reverse Address Resolution Protocol)

_____
_____
_____

Routed protocol

_____
_____
_____

Router

_____
_____
_____

Routing protocol

_____
_____
_____

TCP/IP (Transmission Control Protocol/Internet Protocol)

_____
_____
_____

Focus Questions   Name: _____

Date: _____   Class: _____

1. What are the two addressing schemes in networking?

_____
_____
_____
_____
_____
_____

2. When making forwarding decisions, what type of addresses do routers use?

_____
_____
_____
_____
_____
_____
_____

3. A router's attachment to a network is called an *interface*, which can also be referred to as what?

_____
_____
_____
_____
_____
_____
_____

4. What protocol does a device use to obtain an IP address when it starts up?

_____
_____
_____
_____
_____
_____
_____

5. When devices communicate, what suite is used to automatically detect the MAC address?

_____
_____
_____

6. When a router receives a frame, what happens to the frame header and the IP header?

_____
_____
_____
_____
_____
_____
_____
_____

7. Do most network services use connectionless or connection-oriented delivery systems?

_____
_____
_____
_____
_____
_____
_____
_____

8. What is the difference between EIGRP and IGRP?

_____
_____
_____
_____
_____
_____
_____

9. What is the most common method to transfer routing protocols between routers on the same network?

_____
_____
_____
_____
_____
_____

CCNA Exam Review Questions
The following questions help you review for the CCNA exam. Answers are found in Appendix A, "Answers to the CCNA Exam Review Questions."

1. What is the Address Resolution Protocol (ARP)?
    a. Network protocol used to resolve device conflicts
    b. Internet protocol used to map an IP address to a MAC address
    c. Network protocol used to identify the location of unauthorized users
    d. Internet protocol used to uniquely identify a user on a specific network

2. What must a data packet contain to be passed from the network layer to upper levels of the OSI model?
    a. A destination MAC address and a source IP address
    b. A destination MAC address and a destination IP address
    c. A destination IP address or a source MAC address
    d. Either a destination IP address or a destination MAC address

3. What happens if a data packet lacks a destination IP?
    a. The data packet is sent to the RARP server that traces the data packet back to its source.
    b. The MAC address takes priority and the data packet is passed up to the next network layer.
    c. The ARP tables will be consulted to resolve any conflict.
    d. Data packets will not be passed to the next higher network layer.

4. What happens if a data packet lacks a MAC address?
    a. The data packet is sent to the RARP server that traces the data packet back to its source.
    b. The IP address takes priority and the data packet is passed up to the next higher network layer.
    c. The ARP tables will be consulted to resolve any conflict.
    d. Data packets will not be passed to the next higher network layer.

5. What happens if the ARP table maps the destination IP address to the destination MAC address?
    a. The data packet is sent to the RARP server.
    b. The source broadcasts the IP address to all devices.
    c. The IP address is bound with the MAC address.
    d. The network traffic is reduced and response times decreased.

6. What initiates an ARP request?
    a. A device is unable to locate the destination IP address in its ARP table.
    b. The RARP server in response to a malfunctioning device.
    c. A diskless workstation with an empty cache.
    d. A device is unable to locate the destination MAC address in its ARP table.

7. What happens if a device is unable to locate the destination MAC address in its ARP table?
   a. An ARP request is sent.
   b. The RARP server is consulted.
   c. The destination IP address is used instead.
   d. A data packet is sent to the dummy terminal.

8. What is a header?
   a. IP address of the source device placed at the beginning of the data packet
   b. Route the data packet takes through the network when it follows a predetermined path
   c. Control information placed before data when encapsulating that data for network transmission
   d. Protocol to convert information from one stack to another at the application layer

9. What is a frame?
   a. Logical grouping of information sent as a data link layer unit over a transmission medium
   b. Location where ARP tables are stored on a device
   c. Data packet sent to a diskless workstation
   d. Destination MAC and IP address bound together as a data packet

10. What are the header and trailer referred to as?
    a. Frame
    b. ARP reply
    c. IP address
    d. RARP reply

11. Which best describes the function of a frame?
    a. Binding of MAC and IP addresses
    b. Used for synchronization and error control
    c. Querying of all devices on the network
    d. Consulting the ARP tables to look up addresses

12. What is used for synchronization and error control?
    a. Trailer
    b. Header
    c. Frame
    d. Protocol

13. Which best describes the structure of the ARP request frame?
    a. MAC and IP address
    b. Destination IP address and source IP address
    c. Frame header and ARP message
    d. Addresses and trailer

14. What are the two parts of the frame header called?
    a. MAC header and IP header
    b. Source address and ARP message
    c. Destination address and RARP message
    d. Request and data packet

15. Which best describes RARP?
    a. Finds MAC addresses based on IP addresses
    b. Calculates of shortest route between source and destination
    c. Finds IP addresses based on MAC addresses
    d. Reduces network traffic by maintaining constant contact with all network devices

16. Why is a RARP request made?
    a. A source knows its MAC address but not its IP address.
    b. The data packet needs to find the shortest route between destination and source.
    c. The administrator needs to manually configure the system.
    d. A link in the network faults and a redundant system must be activated.

17. Which of the following devices build ARP tables?
    a. Hubs
    b. Routers
    c. Data links
    d. Encoders

18. Which best defines a gateway?
    a. A network device that has an IP address and maintains ARP tables
    b. A device that connects one network to another network
    c. A device that performs an application layer conversion of information from one stack to another
    d. A device that cleans and amplifies signals

Engineering Journal (Continued)

Chapter 12   Layer 4: The Transport Layer

Introduction

Services located in the transport layer, which is Layer 4 of the OSI reference model, allow users to segment several upper-layer applications onto the same Layer 4 data stream. These services also allow for the reassembly of the same upper-layer application segments at the receiving end.

The Layer 4 data stream provides transport services from the host to the destination. Services such as these are sometimes referred to as end-to-end services. The Layer 4 data stream is a logical connection between the endpoints of a network.

As the transport layer sends its data segments, it can also ensure the integrity of the data. One method of doing this is called *flow control*. Flow control avoids the problem of a host at one side of the connection overflowing the buffers in the host at the other side. Overflows can present serious problems because they can result in data loss.

Transport-layer services also allow users to request reliable data transport between hosts and destinations. To obtain such reliable transport of data, a connection-oriented relationship is used between the communicating end systems. Reliable transport can accomplish the following:

- It ensures that segments delivered will be acknowledged back to the sender.
- It provides for retransmission of any segments that are not acknowledged.
- It puts segments back into their correct sequence at the destination.
- It provides congestion avoidance and control.

Concept Questions

Demonstrate your knowledge of these concepts by answering the following questions in the space provided.

- One user of the transport layer must establish a connection-oriented session with its peer system.

- For data transfer to begin, both the sending and receiving application programs inform their respective operating systems that a connection will be initiated. **How is this accomplished?**

- In concept, one machine places a call that must be accepted by the other. **If the receiving machine does not accept the call, what happens?**

- Protocol software modules in the two operating systems communicate by sending messages. Messages are sent across the network to verify that the transfer is authorized and that both sides are ready. **How is this accomplished?**

- After all synchronization occurrs, a connection is established, and data transfer begins. **How do both machines know that the data is flowing correctly?**

Engineering Journal
In the space provided, answer the Concept Questions.

_____
_____
_____
_____
_____
_____
_____
_____
_____
_____
_____
_____
_____
_____
_____
_____
_____
_____
_____
_____
_____
_____
_____
_____
_____
_____
_____
_____
_____
_____
_____
_____

Vocabulary Exercise Chapter 12   Name: _____

Date: _____   **Class:** _____

Define the following terms as completely as you can. Use the online Chapter 1 or the
Cisco Systems Networking Academy: First-Year Companion Guide, Second Edition,
material for help.

Best-effort delivery

_____

_____

_____

ES (end system)

_____

_____

_____

Flow control

_____

_____

_____

Full duplex

_____

_____

_____

TCP (Transmission Control Protocol)

_____

_____

_____

Transport layer

_____

_____

_____

UDP (User Datagram Protocol)

_____

_____

_____

Window size

_____

_____

_____

Focus Questions   **Name:** _____

Date. _____   **Class:** _____

1. What type of numbers are used to keep track of different conversations that cross the network at the same time?

   _____
   _____
   _____

2. What is the name of a protocol that combines connectionless and connection-oriented service?

   _____
   _____
   _____

3. What is the difference between TCP and UDP?

   _____
   _____
   _____

4. What is the field in a TCP segment that ensures correct sequencing of the arriving data?

   _____
   _____
   _____

5. What are the protocols that use UDP?

   _____
   _____
   _____

6. What range of port numbers is reserved for public applications?

   _____
   _____
   _____

7. What type of a window refers to the fact that the window size is negotiated dynamically during the TCP session?

   _____
   _____
   _____

CCNA Exam Review Questions
The following questions help you prepare for the CCNA Exam. Answers found in
Appendix A, "Answers to the CCNA Exam Review Questions."

1. Which layer of the OSI model provides transport services from the host to the
   destination?
   a. Application
   b. Presentation
   c. Session
   d. Transport

2. Which best describes the function of the transport layer?
   a. Establishes, manages, and terminates applications
   b. Provides transport services from the host to the destination
   c. Supports communication between programs like electronic mail, file transfer,
      and Web browsers
   d. Translates between different data formats such as ASCII and EBCDIC

3. Which method best describes flow control?
   a. A method to manage limited bandwidth
   b. A method of connecting two hosts synchronously
   c. A method to ensure data integrity
   d. A method to check data for viruses prior to transmission

4. Which function best describes flow control?
   a. Checks data packets for integrity and legitimacy prior to transmission
   b. Avoids traffic backup by cycling host quickly through alternate send and
      receive modes during peak traffic periods
   c. Connects two hosts over an exclusive high-speed link for critical data transfer
   d. Avoids the problem of a host at one side of the connection, overflowing the
      buffers in the host at the other side

5. Which of the following occurs in the transport layer when a connection is first
   established between computers in network?
   a. Acknowledgment and retransmission
   b. Encapsulation and broadcasting
   c. Synchronization and acknowledgment
   d. Recovery and flow control

6. Which of the following occurs in the transport layer when data congestion occurs?
   a. Broadcasting
   b. Windowing
   c. Error recovery
   d. Flow control

7. Which layer of the OSI model handles flow control and error recovery?
    a. Application
    b. Presentation
    c. Transport
    d. Network

8. What technique allows multiple applications to share a transport connection?
    a. Broadcasting
    b. Synchronicity
    c. Encapsulation
    d. Segmentation

9. Which best describes segmentation?
    a. Breaks data into smaller packets for faster transmission
    b. Switches hosts from send to receive mode continuously during peak traffic periods
    c. Allows multiple applications to share a transport connection
    d. Transfers data from the presentation layer to the network layer for encoding and encapsulation

10. What method controls the amount of information transferred end-to-end and helps enable TCP reliability?
    a. Broadcasting
    b. Windowing
    c. Error recovery
    d. Flow control

11. If the window size is set to 1, when would an acknowledgment of data packet receipt be sent back to the source?
    a. After one packet
    b. After two packets
    c. After three packets
    d. After four packets

12. If the window size is set to 3, when would an acknowledgment of data packet receipt be sent back to the source?
    a. After one packet
    b. After three packets
    c. After six packets
    d. After nine packets

Chapter 13   Layer 5: The Session Layer

Introduction

The session layer, which is Layer 5 of the OSI reference model, establishes, manages, and terminates sessions between applications. Essentially, the session layer coordinates service requests and responses that occur when applications communicate between different hosts.

Concept Questions

Demonstrate your knowledge of these concepts by answering the following question in the space provided.

- Session layer functions coordinate communication interactions between applications. **Give an example of how these communication interactions are coordinated.**

Engineering Journal
In the space provided, answer the Concept Questions.

_____

_____

_____

_____

_____

_____

_____

_____

_____

_____

_____

_____

_____

_____

_____

_____

_____

_____

_____

_____

_____

_____

_____

Vocabulary Exercise Chapter 13   **Name:**_____

Date:_____   **Class:**_____

Define the following terms as completely as you can. Use the online Chapter 13 or the *Cisco Systems Networking Academy: First-Year Companion Guide*, Second Edition, material for help.

Collision

_____

_____

_____

Protocol

_____

_____

_____

Session

_____

_____

_____

Session layer

_____

_____

_____

TWS (two-way simultaneous)

_____

_____

_____

Focus Questions   **Name:** _____

Date: _____   **Class:** _____

1. Which of the following are Layer 5 protocols?
    a. (NFS)Network File System
    b. (SQL)Structured Query Language
    c. (RPC)Remote Procedure Call
    d. X-Window System
    e. (ASP)AppleTalk Session Protocol
    f. DNA (Digital Network Architecture)
    g. SCP (Session Control Protocol)

2. In a session, checkpoints used for what?

    _____
    _____
    _____

3. What is dialogue separation?

    _____
    _____
    _____

4. When in the session layer, what are the responsibilities of both hosts when sending a message?

    _____
    _____
    _____

5. What type of two-way communication is the session layer most involved in?

    _____
    _____
    _____

6. What is the responsibility of the session layer?

    _____
    _____
    _____

7. When computers communicate with each other, what is the dialogue process called that determines which computer takes on the role of the client and which takes on the role of the server?

    _____
    _____
    _____

CCNA Exam Review Questions

The following questions help you review for the CCNA exam. Answers are found in Appendix A, "Answers to the CCNA Exam Review Questions."

1. Which layer of the OSI model establishes, manages, and terminates communication between applications?
    a. Application
    b. Presentation
    c. Session
    d. Transport

2. Which best describes the function of session layer?
    a. Establishes, manages, and terminates communications between applications
    b. Supports communication between programs like electronic mail, file transfer, and Web browsers
    c. Provides transport services from the host to the destination
    d. Translates between different data formats such as ASCII and EBCDIC

Chapter 14   Layer 6: The Presentation Layer

Introduction

Layer 6 of the OSI reference model, the presentation layer, provides code formatting and conversion. Code formatting is used to make sure that applications have meaningful information to process. If necessary, this layer can translate between different data formats.

The presentation layer is not only concerned with the format and representation of data. It is also concerned with the data structure that the programs used. Thus, Layer 6 arranges for Layer 7 how data will be organized when it is transferred.

Concept Questions

Demonstrate your knowledge of these concepts by answering the following questions in the space provided.

- Layer 6 standards also guide how graphic images are presented. **What standards for graphic images do Layer 6 employ?** For example, PICT, a picture format used to transfer QuickDraw graphics between Macintosh and PowerPC programs, can be used. Another presentation format that can be used is the tagged image file format, or TIFF. Typically, TIFF is used for high-resolution, bit-mapped images. Another Layer 6 standard that can be used for graphic images is from the Joint Photographic Experts Group, which is generally referred to as JPEG. **Explain how Layer 6 structures the data for Layer 7 to transfer.**

Engineering Journal
In the space provided, answer the Concept Questions.

Vocabulary Exercise Chapter 14   **Name:** _____

Date: _____   **Class:** _____

Define the following terms as completely as you can. Use the online Chapter 14 or the *Cisco Systems Networking Academy: First-Year Companion Guide*, Second Edition, material for help.

ASCII (American Standard Code for Information Interchange)

_____

_____

_____

Compression

_____

_____

_____

EBCDIC (Extended Binary Coded Decimal Interchange Code)

_____

_____

_____

Encryption

_____

_____

_____

Presentation layer

_____

_____

_____

Focus Questions   Name: _____

Date: _____   Class: _____

1. What are the three functions of the presentation layer?

_____

_____

_____

2. At the receiving station, from which layer does the presentation layer get the data?

_____

_____

_____

3. What types of computers most often use EBCDIC?

_____

_____

_____

4. What is a JPEG?

_____

_____

_____

5. In the presentation layer, what does the algorithm search for to help shrink the size of a file?

_____

_____

_____

6. What type of program uses binary files?

_____

_____

_____

7. What are the two file formats used by the Internet to display images?

_____

_____

_____

8. What type of file format is used as a set of directions for displaying a page on a Web browser?

_____

_____

_____

CCNA Exam Review Questions

The following questions help you review for the CCNA exam. Answers are found in Appendix A, "Answers to the CCNA Exam Review Questions."

1. Which layer of the OSI model layer can translate between different data formats, such as ASCII and EBCDIC?
   a. Application
   b. Presentation
   c. Session
   d. Transport

2. Which layer of the OSI model layer guides how graphic images, sound, and video are presented?
   a. Application
   b. Presentation
   c. Session
   d. Transport

3. Which best describes the function of the presentation layer?
   a. Establishes, manages, and terminates applications
   b. Supports communication between programs like electronic mail, file transfer, and Web browsers
   c. Guides how graphic images, sound, and video are handled
   d. Provides transport services from the host to the destination

4. Which best describes the function of the presentation layer?
   a. Establishes, manages, and terminates applications
   b. Supports communication between programs like electronic mail, file transfer, and Web browsers
   c. Provides transport services from the host to the destination
   d. Translates between different data formats such as ASCII and EBCDIC

5. Which layer of the OSI model layer handles data encryption?
   a. Application
   b. Presentation
   c. Session
   d. Transport

6. ASCII, encryption, QuickTime, JPEG are all typical of which layer?
   a. Presentation
   b. Transport
   c. Application
   d. Session

Chapter 15   Layer 7: The Application Layer

Introduction
In the context of the OSI reference model, the application layer, Layer 7 of the OSI reference model, supports the communicating component of an application.

A computer application can require only information that resides on its computer. However, a network application might have a communicating component from one or more network applications.

A word processor might incorporate a file transfer component that allows a document to be transferred electronically over a network. This file-transfer component qualifies the word processor as an application in the OSI context and belongs in Layer 7 of the OSI reference model.

Web browsers, such as Netscape Navigator and Internet Explorer, also have data transfer components. An example of this is when you go to a Web site—the Web pages are transferred to your computer.

Concept Questions

Demonstrate your knowledge of these concepts by answering the following questions in the space provided.

- The application layer (Layer 7) provides services to application processes that are outside of the OSI model. **What services are provided?**

- The application layer identifies and establishes the availability of intended communication partners and the resources required to connect with them. **What are these resources?**

Engineering Journal
In the space provided, answer the Concept Questions.

_____
_____
_____
_____
_____
_____
_____
_____

Engineering Journal (Continued)

Vocabulary Exercise Chapter 15　　　　Name: _____

Date: _____　　　　Class: _____

Define the following terms as completely as you can. Use the online Chapter 15 or the *Cisco Systems Networking Academy: First-Year Companion Guide*, Second Edition, material for help.

Application layer

_____
_____
_____

Client

_____
_____
_____

Client-server computing

_____
_____
_____

DNS (Domain Name System)

_____
_____
_____

Domain Server

_____
_____
_____

FTP (File Transfer Protocol)

_____
_____
_____

HTML (Hypertext Markup Language)

_____
_____
_____

Hypertext

_____
_____
_____

IP address

_____
_____
_____

Redirector

_____
_____
_____

Server

_____
_____
_____

Telnet

_____
_____
_____

URL (Universal Resource Locator)

_____
_____
_____

Focus Questions   **Name:** _____

Date: _____   **Class:** _____

1. To which other OSI layers does the application layer provide service?

   _____
   _____
   _____

2. What is a network application that uses the direct interface provided by the application layer?

   _____
   _____
   _____

3. What is a network application that uses the indirect interface provided by the application layer?

   _____
   _____
   _____

4. Where is the server side of a client-server application located?

   _____
   _____
   _____

5. What is the looped routine constantly repeated by a client-server application?

   _____
   _____
   _____

6. What does DNS do?

   _____
   _____
   _____

7. Which protocol do File Utility Programs use to copy and move files between remote sites?

   _____
   _____
   _____

8. Which protocol do Remote Access Programs use to directly connect to remote resources?

   _____
   _____
   _____

CCNA Exam Review Questions

The following questions help you prepare for the CCNA Exam. Answers found in Appendix A, "Answers to the CCNA Exam Review Questions."

1. Which layer of the OSI model supports communication between programs, such as e-mail, file transfer, and Web browsers?
   a. Application
   b. Presentation
   c. Session
   d. Transport

2. Which best describes the function of the application layer?
   a. Establishes, manages, and terminates applications
   b. Supports communication between programs like e- mail, file transfer, and Web browsers
   c. Provides transport services from the host to the destination
   d. Translates between different data formats such as ASCII and EBCDIC

3. Which is a network application?
   a. E-mail
   b. Word processor
   c. Web browser
   d. Spreadsheet

4. Which is a computer application?
   a. Remote access
   b. File transfer
   c. Web browser
   d. E-mail

5. E-mail and file transfer are typical functions of which layer in the OSI model?
   a. Transport
   b. Network
   c. Application
   d. Presentation

Chapter 16   WANs and Routers

Introduction

One major characteristic of a wide-area network (WAN) is that the network operates beyond the local LAN's geographic scope. It uses the services of carriers, such as regional Bell operating companies (RBOCs), Sprint, and MCI.

WANs use serial connections of various types to access bandwidth over wide-area geographies. By definition, the WAN connects devices separated by wide areas. WAN devices include the following:

- Routers, which offer many services, including internetworking and WAN interface ports
- Switches, which connect to WAN bandwidth for voice, data, and video communication
- Modems, which interface voice-grade services and channel service units/digital service units
- CSU/DSUs that interface T1/E1 services and Terminal Adapters/Network Termination 1
- TA/NT1s that interface Integrated Services Digital Network (ISDN) services
- Communication servers, which concentrate on dial-in and dial-out user communication

Concept Questions

Demonstrate your knowledge of these concepts by answering the following questions in the space provided.

- A WAN is used to interconnect local-area networks (LANs) that are typically separated by a large geographic area.

- A WAN operates at the OSI reference model physical and data link layers.

- The WAN provides for the exchange of data packets/frames between routers/bridges and the LANs that they support. **Draw a WAN that includes three LANs.**

- **Compare and contrast WANs and LANs layer by layer.**

Engineering Journal
In the space provided, answer the Concept Questions.

_____

_____

_____

_____

Engineering Journal (Continued)

Vocabulary Exercise Chapter 16　　　　　Name: _____

Date: _____　　　　　Class: _____

Define the following terms as completely as you can.

CSU

_____
_____
_____

DCE

_____
_____
_____

DSU

_____
_____
_____

DTE

_____
_____
_____

E1

_____
_____
_____

Frame Relay

_____
_____
_____

HDLC

_____
_____
_____

ISDN

_____

_____

_____

PPP

_____

_____

_____

PTT

_____

_____

_____

RBOC

_____

_____

_____

T1

_____

_____

_____

Focus Questions   **Name:** _____

Date: _____   **Class:** _____

1. Name and briefly describe four WAN devices.

    _____

    _____

    _____

    _____

    _____

    _____

    _____

    _____

2. Name two ways in which WANs differ from LANs.

    _____

    _____

    _____

    _____

    _____

3. What do the acronyms DTE and DCE stand for?

    _____

    _____

    _____

    _____

    _____

4. List three WAN physical layer standards.

    _____

    _____

    _____

    _____

5. List four WAN data link layer protocols.

    _____

    _____

    _____

    _____

    _____

CCNA Exam Review Questions

The following questions help you review for the CCNA exam. Answers are found in Appendix A, "Answers to the CCNA Exam Review Questions."

1. Which of the following best describes a WAN?
    a. Connects LANs that are separated by a large geographic area
    b. Connects workstations, terminals, and other devices in a metropolitan area
    c. Connects LANs within a large building
    d. Connects workstations, terminals, and other devices within a building

2. Which of the following are examples of WANs?
    a. Token Ring and ARCNet
    b. Frame Relay and SMDS
    c. Star and Banyan VINES
    d. CSU/DSU and ARCView

3. What service does a WAN provide to LANs?
    a. High-speed multiple access to data networks
    b. IP addressing and secure data transfer
    c. Exchanging data packets between routers and the LANs those routers support
    d. Direct routing with error checking

4. What type of connections do WANs use that LANs typically do not use?
    a. Parallel, lower speed
    b. Multiple, higher speed
    c. Multiple, lower speed
    d. Serial, lower speed

5. At which layers of the OSI model does a WAN operate?
    a. Physical and application
    b. Physical and data link
    c. Data link and network
    d. Data link and presentation

6. Which layers of the OSI models do WAN standards describe?
    a. Data link and network
    b. Data link and presentation
    c. Physical and application
    d. Physical and data link

7. How do WANs differ from LANs?
    a. Typically exist in defined geographic areas
    b. Provide high-speed multiple access services
    c. Use tokens to regulate network traffic
    d. Use services of common carriers

8. How do WANs differ from LANs?
   a. Emphasize access over serial interfaces operating at lower speeds
   b. Provide high-speed multiple access services
   c. Typically exist in defined geographic areas
   d. Use tokens to regulate network traffic

9. How are operational and functional connections for WANs obtained?
   a. From your local telephone company
   b. From InterNIC
   c. From regional Bell operating companies (RBOC)
   d. From the WWW Consortium

10. What do the WAN physical layer standards describe?
    a. Interface between SDLC and HDLC
    b. How frames are sent and verified
    c. How voice and data traffic are routed
    d. Interface between DTE and DCE

11. Which best describes what WAN data link protocols define?
    a. How frames are carried between systems on a single data link
    b. Methods for determining optimum path to a destination
    c. How data packets are transmitted between systems on multiple data links
    d. Methods for mapping IP addresses to MAC addresses

12. Which is a WAN data link protocol?
    a. TCP/IP
    b. Point-to-point
    c. EIGRP
    d. OSPF

13. Which is a WAN data link protocol?
    a. TCP/IP
    b. OSPF
    c. EIGRP
    d. Frame Relay

14. Which best describes data terminal equipment (DTE)?
    a. Physical connection between networks and users
    b. Generates clocking signals to control network traffic
    c. Device at the user end of a network
    d. Physical devices such as modems and interface cards

15. Which is an example of data terminal equipment (DTE)?
    a. Interface card
    b. Modem
    c. Computer
    d. CSU/DSU

16. Which best describes data circuit terminating equipment (DCE)?
    a. Device at the user end of a network
    b. Serves as data source and/or destination
    c. Physical devices such as protocol translators and multiplexers
    d. Physical connection between networks and users

17. Which is an example of data circuit terminating equipment (DCE)?
    a. Multiplexer
    b. Modem
    c. Translator
    d. Computer

18. Which best describes High-Level Data Link Control (HDLC)?
    a. Digital service that transmits voice and data over existing phone lines
    b. Uses high-quality digital facilities—fastest WAN protocol
    c. Provides router-to-router and host-to-network connections over synchronous and asynchronous circuits
    d. Supports point-to-point and multipoint configurations, and uses frame characters and checksums

19. Which WAN protocol can be described as supporting point-to-point and multipoint configurations?
    a. HDLC
    b. Frame Relay
    c. PPP
    d. ISDN

20. Which WAN protocol can be described as using frame characters and checksums?
    a. ISDN
    b. Frame Relay
    c. PPP
    d. HDLC

21. Which best describes Frame Relay?
    a. Uses high-quality digital facilities—fastest WAN protocol
    b. Supports point-to-point and multipoint configurations, and uses frame characters and checksums
    c. Digital service that transmits voice and data over existing telephone lines
    d. Provides router-to-router and host-to-network connections over synchronous and asynchronous circuits

22. Which WAN protocol can be described as using high-quality digital facilities?
   a. HDLC
   b. Frame Relay
   c. PPP
   d. ISDN

23. Which WAN protocol can be described as the fastest WAN protocol?
   a. HDLC
   b. PPP
   c. Frame Relay
   d. ISDN

24. Which best describes PPP?
   a. Uses high-quality digital facilities—fastest WAN protocol
   b. Supports point-to-point and multipoint configurations, and uses frame characters and checksums
   c. Provides router-to-router and host-to-network connections over synchronous and asynchronous circuits
   d. Digital service that transmits voice and data over existing telephone lines

25. Which WAN protocol can be described as providing router-to-router and host-to-network connections over synchronous and asynchronous circuits?
   a. HDLC
   b. Frame Relay
   c. PPP
   d. ISDN

26. Which best describes ISDN?
   a. Digital service that transmits voice and data over existing phone lines
   b. Provides router-to-router and host-to-network connections over synchronous and asynchronous circuits
   c. Uses high quality digital facilities—fastest WAN protocol
   d. Supports point-to-point and multipoint configurations, and uses frame characters and checksums

27. Which WAN protocol can be described as a digital service that transmits voice and data over existing telephone lines?
   a. HDLC
   b. Frame Relay
   c. PPP
   d. ISDN

Chapter 17   Router CLI

Introduction
You configure Cisco routers from the user interface that runs on the router console or terminal. You can also configure Cisco routers by using remote access. You must log in to the router before you can enter an EXEC command.

For security purposes, the router has two levels of access to commands:

- **User mode**—Typical tasks include those that check the router status. In this mode, router configuration changes are not allowed.

- **Privileged mode**—Typical tasks include those that change the router configuration.

Concept Questions

Demonstrate your knowledge of these concepts by answering the following questions in the space provided.

- You can use the router to do the following:
    Log in with the user password
    Enter privileged mode with the enable password
    Disable or quit
    What procedures would you follow to log in to the router?

- You can use the following advanced help features:
    Command completion and prompting
    Syntax checking
    Why would you need to use syntax checking?

- You can use the following advanced editing features:
    Automatic line scrolling
    Cursor controls
    History buffer with command recall
    Copy and paste, which are available on most laptop computers
    Why is it important to have two access of commands?

Engineering Journal
In the space provided, answer the Concept Questions.

_____
_____
_____
_____
_____

Engineering Journal (Continued)

Vocabulary Exercise Chapter 17   Name: _____

Date: _____   **Class:** _____

Define the following terms as completely as you can.

Privileged mode

_____
_____
_____

User mode

_____
_____
_____

Focus Questions   **Name:** _____

Date: _____   **Class:** _____

1. How do you use a router?

    _____
    _____
    _____

2. Distinguish between user mode and privileged mode.

    _____
    _____
    _____

3. In Cisco IOS, what is the user mode prompt and what is the privileged mode prompt?

    _____
    _____
    _____

4. What must you type at the user or privileged mode prompts to display a list of
    commonly used commands?

    _____
    _____
    _____

5. When in user mode, what must you do to enter privileged mode?

    _____
    _____
    _____

6. If you are unsure of the syntax or arguments for a command, what feature can be of
    great help to you?

    _____
    _____
    _____

CCNA Exam Review Questions

The following questions help you review for the CCNA exam. Answers are found in Appendix A, "Answers to the CCNA Exam Review Questions."

1. What are the two modes of access to router commands for Cisco routers?
    a. User and privileged
    b. User and guest
    c. Privileged and guest
    d. Guest and anonymous

2. Why are there two modes of access to router commands on Cisco routers?
    a. One mode is for remotely working on the router, while the other mode is for directly working on the router via a console.
    b. One mode, which has many automatic sequences, is for new users, while the other mode is for experienced users who can issue direct commands.
    c. One mode lets a number of users see what's happening on the router, while the other mode lets a few users change how the router operates.
    d. One mode is for the initial router configuration and startup, while the other mode is for maintaining, updating, and changing the router after initial startup.

3. What can be done only in privileged mode on Cisco routers?
    a. Change the configuration
    b. Enter commands
    c. Check routing tables
    d. Monitor performance

4. How do you switch from user to privileged mode on Cisco routers?
    a. Type **admin** and enter a password.
    b. Type **root** and enter a password.
    c. Type **enable** and enter a password.
    d. Type **privileged** and enter a password.

5. What happens if you type **enable** on a Cisco router user interface?
    a. You switch to user mode.
    b. The last command entered is activated.
    c. A new LAN is added to the router table.
    d. You switch to privileged mode.

6. Which of the commands is *not* available in the user access mode?
    a. **show**
    b. **ppp**
    c. **trace**
    d. **ping**

7. Which is the user-mode prompt for Cisco router user interfaces?
    a. #
    b. >
    c. <
    d. |#

8. Which is the privileged mode prompt for Cisco router user interfaces?
    a. #
    b. >
    c. <
    d. |#

9. How do you log out of a Cisco router user interface?
    a. Type **Control-Q**
    b. Type **quit**
    c. Type **exit**
    d. Type **Control-X**

10. How can you get a list of commonly used commands from a Cisco router user interface?
    a. Type **list**
    b. Type **Control-C**
    c. Type **Control-?**
    d. Type **?**

11. What does the "More" prompt at the bottom of a screen on a Cisco router user interface mean?
    a. Multiple screens are available as output.
    b. Additional detail is available in the manual pages.
    c. Multiple entries are required in the command.
    d. Additional conditions must be stated.

12. How do you get to the next screen if "More" is indicated at the bottom of the current screen on a Cisco router user interface?
    a. Press the Page Down key.
    b. Press the Spacebar.
    c. Press the End key.
    d. Press the Tab key.

13. Which keystroke(s) automatically repeat(s) the previous command entry on a Cisco router user interface?
    a. Left arrow
    b. Right arrow
    c. Control-R
    d. Control-P

14. What happens if you type **?** in a Cisco router user interface?
  a. You see all users logged into the router.
  b. You list the last command you typed.
  c. You enter the Help system.
  d. You find out which mode you are currently in.

15. What does it mean if you see the symbol ^ on a Cisco router user interface?
  a. Indicates location of an error in a command string
  b. Indicates that you are in Help mode
  c. Indicates that more information must be entered to complete the command
  d. Indicates that you are in privileged mode

16. What would you type at the router user prompt if you want to see what show subcommands are available?
  a. **?**
  b. **Command ?**
  c. **Show ?**
  d. **List ?**

17. What would you type at the router user prompt if you wanted to see what configuration subcommands are available?
  a. **?**
  b. **Command ?**
  c. **List ?**
  d. **Config ?**

18. What command is only available at the privileged access mode?
  a. **ping**
  b. **show**
  c. **trace**
  d. **ppp**

Engineering Journal (Continued)

Chapter 18   Router Components

Introduction
Whether accessed from the console or by a Telnet session through an auxiliary port, the router can be placed in several modes. Each mode provides different functions:

- **User EXEC mode**—A "look-only" mode where the user can view some information about the router, but cannot change anything.
- **Privileged EXEC mode**—Supports the debugging and testing commands, detailed examination of the router, manipulation of configuration files, and access to configuration modes.
- **Setup mode**—Presents an interactive prompted dialog box at the console that helps the new user create a first-time, basic configuration.
- **Global configuration mode**—Implements powerful one-line commands that perform simple configuration tasks.
- **Other configuration modes**—Provide more complicated multiple-line configurations.
- **RXBOOT mode**—A maintenance mode that can be used, among other things, to recover lost passwords.

Concept Questions

Demonstrate your knowledge of these concepts by answering the following questions in the space provided.

- The router is made up of configurable components. **How are these components configured?**

- The router has modes for examining, maintaining, and changing the components. **In the examining mode, what does the router do?**

- Show commands are used for examination. **What does the show command examine?**

- Use CDP to show entries about neighbors.

- Access other routers with Telnet.

- Test network connectivity layer by layer. Testing commands include **ping**, **trace**, and **debug. What is the difference between trace and ping?**

Engineering Journal
In the space provided, answer the Concept Questions.

Vocabulary Exercise Chapter 18　　　　Name: _____

Date: _____　　　　Class: _____

Define the following terms as completely as you can.

CDP

_____
_____
_____

CPU

_____
_____
_____

DRAM

_____
_____
_____

Interface

_____
_____
_____

NVRAM

_____
_____
_____

Ping

_____
_____
_____

RAM

_____
_____
_____

Telnet

_____
_____
_____

TFTP

_____
_____
_____

Trace

_____
_____
_____

Focus Questions   Name: _____

Date: _____   **Class:** _____

1. Diagram the internal components (subsystems) of a modern multimedia PC. Diagram the external features of a modern multimedia PC.

2. List three external configuration sources for Cisco routers.

   _____
   _____
   _____

3. List and describe the internally configurable components of a router.

   _____
   _____
   _____

4. List at least seven commands that can show router status and the configurable components they display information about.

   _____
   _____
   _____

5. Briefly describe what Cisco Discovery Protocol (CDP) **show cdp neighbors** can tell you about a network.

   _____
   _____
   _____

6. Using the OSI model and the commands **telnet, ping, trace, show ip route**, and **show interface**, describe the basic testing of a network.

   _____
   _____
   _____

CCNA Exam Review Questions

The following questions help you review for the CCNA exam. Answers are found in Appendix A, "Answers to the CCNA Exam Review Questions."

1. Which of the following describes a location from which a router is configured?
    a. After it's installed on the network, a router can be configured from virtual terminals.
    b. Upon initial configuration, a router is configured from the virtual terminals.
    c. After it's installed on the network, a router can be configured via modem from the console terminal.
    d. Upon initial configuration, a router is configured via modem using the auxiliary port.

2. Which of the following does *not* describe external configuration of routers?
    a. Upon initial configuration, a router is configured from the console terminal.
    b. The router can be connected via modem using the console port.
    c. After it's installed, a router is configured from the console terminal.
    d. Configuration files can be downloaded from a TFTP server on the network.

3. Which of the following router components has these characteristics: Stores routing tables, fast-switching cache, and packet hold queues?
    a. NVRAM
    b. RAM/DRAM
    c. Flash
    d. ROM

4. Which of the following router components has these characteristics: holds the operating system and microcode; retains its contents when you power down or restart; and allows software updates without replacing chips?
    a. NVRAM
    b. RAM/DRAM
    c. Flash
    d. ROM

5. Which of the following best describes the function of NVRAM?
    a. Provides temporary and/or running memory for the router's configuration file while the router is powered on.
    b. Stores the router's backup configuration file. The content is retained when you power down or restart.
    c. Holds the operating system image and microcode and allows you to update software without removing and replacing chips on the processor.
    d. Contains power-on diagnostics, a bootstrap program, and operating system software.

6. Which of the following does *not* describe a function of working storage RAM in a router?
    a. A bootstrap program performs tests and then loads the Cisco IOS software into memory.
    b. A saved version of the configuration file is accessed from NVRAM and loaded into main memory when the router initializes.
    c. The EXEC part of the IOS software handles packet buffering and the queuing of packets.
    d. The operating system image is usually executed from the main RAM and loaded from an input source.

7. Which of the following is the router mode that supports debugging and testing commands, manipulation of configuration files, and detailed examination of the router?
    a. Global configuration mode
    b. RXBOOT mode
    c. Privileged EXEC mode
    d. Setup mode

8. Which of the following describes functions of the user EXEC mode of a router?
    a. Presents an interactive prompted dialog that helps the new user create a first-time basic configuration
    b. Implements powerful one-line commands that perform simple configuration tasks
    c. Used for recovery from catastrophe, such as to recover lost passwords
    d. Allows the user to view some information about the router but not change anything

9. If you are in global configuration mode, what does the router prompt look like?
    a. router #
    b. router (config) #
    c. router-config #
    d. r-config #

10. When you are in user mode, what does the router prompt look like?
    a. router -
    b. router >
    c. router #
    d. router

11. What is the command you enter to gain access to privileged EXEC mode?
    a. **ena**
    b. **p exec**
    c. **exec**
    d. **enable p-exec**

12. Which of the following does *not* correctly describe the function of a router status command?
    a. **show version**—Displays configuration of the system hardware, the names and sources of configuration files, and the boot images.
    b. **show mem**—Displays statistics about the router's memory, including memory free pool statistics.
    c. **show buffers**—Displays statistics for the buffer pools on the router.
    d. **show interfaces**—Displays statistics for all interfaces configured on the router.

13. If you type **show ?** at the router > prompt, what appears on the screen?
    a. Nothing, this is not a valid command.
    b. All the items that can be shown in user mode.
    c. The status of the router.
    d. Information about the version of the IOS that is currently running.

14. Which of the following describes a function of the **show running-config** Cisco IOS command?
    a. It allows an administrator to see the image size and startup configuration commands the router will use on the next restart.
    b. It displays a message at the top showing how much nonvolatile memory has been used.
    c. It allows an administrator to see the configuration of the processes and interrupt routines.
    d. It allows an administrator to see the current running configuration on the router.

15. Which of the following describes a function of the **show startup-config** Cisco IOS command?
    a. It allows an administrator to see the current running configuration on the router.
    b. It displays a message at the top showing how much nonvolatile memory has been used.
    c. It allows an administrator to see the reason for the last system reboot.
    d. It displays this message at the top: "Current Configuration".

16. The **show interface serial** Cisco IOS router command can display which one of the following lines of information?
    a. IOS (tm) 4500 Software (C4500-J-M), Experimental Version 11.2.
    b. DECNET routing is enabled.
    c. Serial1 is up, line protocol is up.
    d. System image file is "c4500-j-mz".

17. The **show version** Cisco IOS router command can display which one of the following lines of information?
    a. IOS (tm) 4500 Software (C4500-J-M), Experimental Version 11.2.
    b. Hardware is MK5025.
    c. Internet Protocol routing is enabled.
    d. Internet address is 183.8.64.129.

18. The **show protocols** Cisco IOS router command can display which one of the following lines of information?
    a. Serial1 is up, line protocol is up.
    b. Compiled Fri 28-Jun-96.
    c. AppleTalk routing is enabled.
    d. ROM; System Bootstrap, Version 5.1(1).

19. What kind of information *cannot* be obtained when you enter **show interface** in the user mode?
    a. The MAC address for all interfaces
    b. The IP address for all interfaces
    c. How many users are logged onto each interface
    d. The encapsulation protocol for each interface

20. If you type **show interface E0** at the prompt router#, which of the following best shows what the first five lines of the response would look like if the interface was up?
    a. Ethernet0 is up, line protocol is up
       Address is 0000.0f92.c54b (bia 0000.0f92.c54b)
       Internet address is 223.8.151.1/24
       MTU 1500 bytes, BW 10000 Kbit, DLY 1000 usec, rely 255/255, load 1/255
       Encapsulation ARPA, loopback not set, keepalive set (10sec)

    b. Ethernet0 is up, line protocol is up
       Hardware is Lance, address is 0000.0f92.c54b (bia 0000.0f92.c54b)
       Internet address is 223.8.151.1/24
       ARP type: ARPA, ARP Timeout 05:00:00
       Encapsulation ARPA, loopback not set, keepalive set (10sec)

    c. Ethernet0 is up, line protocol is up
       Hardware is Lance, address is 0000.0f92.c54b (bia 0000.0f92.c54b)
       Internet address is 223.8.151.1/24
       MTU 1500 bytes, BW 10000 Kbit, DLY 1000 usec, rely 255/255, load 1/255
       Encapsulation ARPA, loopback not set, keepalive set (10sec)

    d. Ethernet0 is up, line protocol is up
       Address is 0000.0f92.c54b (bia 0000.0f92.c54b)
       Internet address is 223.8.151.1/24
       Subnet Mask is 255.255.255.255/24
       Encapsulation ARPA, loopback not set, keepalive set (10sec)

21. Which one of the following is a function of Cisco Discovery Protocol (CDP)?
    a. Provides a way to use an echo to evaluate the path-to-host reliability
    b. Provides a way to determine whether a routing table entry exists
    c. Provides a way to see the current running configuration on the local router
    d. Provides a way to access summaries of configurations on directly connected devices

22. Which of the following is a characteristic of Cisco Discovery Protocol (CDP)?
    a. It runs over OSI Layer 3.
    b. It allows CDP devices that support different network-layer protocols to learn about each other.
    c. It obtains information about neighboring devices only if the administrator enters commands.
    d. It obtains information only about devices running TCP/IP.

23. What steps does the network administrator have to take to make Cisco Discovery Protocol (CDP) run at system start up?
    a. Type **cdp enable** at the first router prompt.
    b. Type **cdp enable** at the first privilege EXEC router prompt.
    c. CDP runs automatically at start up.
    d. Type **cdp enable** at any prompt at then save the config file.

24. Which of the following is a function of the CDP **show** command?
    a. It displays information about any CDP-enabled router on the network.
    b. It displays information on a console connected to any node in the network.
    c. It helps evaluate delays over network paths and path-to-host reliability.
    d. It identifies neighboring routers' host names and IP addresses.

25. Which of the following is *not* provided by the CDP **show** command to tell about neighbor routers?
    a. Processes list, with information about the active processes
    b. Port identifier, such as Ethernet0, Serial1, etc.
    c. The device's hardware platform
    d. Address list, with addresses for supported protocols

26. Which of the following is a function of the **cdp enable** command?
    a. Boots up the Cisco IOS software and implements diagnostic testing
    b. Displays values of the CDP timers
    c. Begins CDP's dynamic discovery function on the router's interfaces
    d. Discards expired holdtime values

27. Which of the following is *not* a function of the **show cdp interface** command?
    a. Displays the values of the CDP timers
    b. Displays the reasons for system reboot
    c. Displays the interface status
    d. Displays the encapsulation used by CDP

28. Which of the following is a function of the **show cdp entry** {*device name*} command?
    a. Establishes a connection to a remote router
    b. Displays the cached CDP entry for every directly connected CDP router
    c. Allows an administrator to see the IP addresses of the targeted router
    d. Displays version information about the network protocols running on the router

29. Which of the following is *not* a function of the **show cdp entry** {*device name*} command?
    a. Displays the cached CDP entry for every directly connected CDP router
    b. Displays all Layer 3 addresses present on the router
    c. Displays how long ago the CDP frame arrived from the router
    d. Displays version information about the router

30. Which of the following is a function of the **show cdp neighbors** command?
    a. Displays the device capability code of remote routers
    b. Displays the path-to-host reliability of a network connection
    c. Displays the encapsulation of the protocols used by neighbor routers
    d. Displays the neighbor's remote port type and number

31. Which of the following is *not* a function of the **show cdp neighbors** command?
    a. Displays the cached CDP entry for every directly connected CDP router
    b. Displays the CDP updates received on any network router
    c. Displays information like that from **show cdp entry** when **show cdp neighbors detail** is used
    d. Displays neighbor device IDs

32. Why would you use the **show cdp neighbors** command?
    a. To get a snapshot view of the routers in the network
    b. To get a overview of the routers that are directly connected to me
    c. To get the IP addresses for neighboring routers
    d. To building a routing table for all routers in the network neighborhood

33. Which of the following is a feature of Telnet router operations?
    a. Telnet is typically used to connect a router to neighbor routers.
    b. A router can have only one incoming Telnet session at a time.
    c. A Telnet session can be suspended and then resumed.
    d. To initiate a Telnet session, you have to know the name of the host.

Chapter 19   Router Startup and Setup

Introduction

The startup routines for Cisco IOS software have the goal of starting router operations. The router must deliver reliable performance connecting the user networks it was configured to serve. To do this, the startup routines must do the following:

- Make sure that the router comes up with all its hardware tested.
- Find from memory and load the Cisco IOS software that the router uses for its operating system.
- Find from memory and apply the configuration statements about the router, including protocol functions and interface addresses.

The router makes sure that it comes up with tested hardware. When a Cisco router powers up, it performs a power-up self-test. During this self-test, the router executes diagnostics from ROM on all modules. These diagnostics verify the basic operation of the CPU, memory, and network interface ports. After it verifies the hardware functions, the router proceeds with software initialization.

Concept Questions

Demonstrate your knowledge of these concepts by answering the following questions in the space provided.

- The router initializes by loading a bootstrap, the operating system, and a configuration file. **What does each of these items do?**

- If the router cannot find a configuration file, the router enters setup mode. **What does the setup mode do?**

- The router stores a backup copy of the new configuration from setup mode. **Where does the router store this backup copy?**

- **Flowchart the startup (boot) sequence of a multimedia PC.**

Engineering Journal
In the space provided, answer the Concept Questions.

_____
_____
_____
_____
_____
_____
_____

Engineering Journal (Continued)

Vocabulary Exercise Chapter 19   **Name:** _____

Date: _____   **Class:** _____

Define the following terms as completely as you can.

CPU

_____
_____
_____

Erase startup-config

_____
_____
_____

Reload

_____
_____
_____

Focus Questions

Date: _____

Name: _____

Class: _____

1. What are the three main things the router accomplishes upon startup?

    _____

    _____

    _____

    _____

    _____

    _____

2. Briefly describe the router startup sequence.

    _____

    _____

    _____

    _____

    _____

    _____

3. What is the main purpose of setup mode?

    _____

    _____

    _____

    _____

    _____

    _____

4. During the System Configuration Dialog, you are prompted to set up "global parameters" and to set up "interfaces." Explain.

    _____

    _____

    _____

5. After you complete the setup command program and your configuration is displayed, you are asked if you want to use this configuration. If you answer yes, what happens?

    _____

    _____

    _____

    _____

    _____

    _____

CCNA Exam Review Questions

The following questions help you review for the CCNA exam. Answers are found in Appendix A, "Answers to the CCNA Exam Review Questions."

1. Which of the following is the correct order of steps in the Cisco router system startup routine?
    a. (1) locate and load operating system, (2) load bootstrap, (3) test hardware, (4) locate and load configuration file
    b. (1) test hardware, (2) load bootstrap, (3) locate and load operating system, (4) locate and load configuration file
    c. (1) load bootstrap, (2) locate and load configuration file, (3) test hardware, (4) locate and load operating system
    d. (1) test hardware, (2) load bootstrap, (3) locate and load configuration file, (4) locate and load operating system

2. Which of the following is *not* a step in the Cisco router system startup routine?
    a. Load bootstrap
    b. Power-up hardware self-test
    c. Enable CDP on each interface
    d. Locate and load configuration file

3. Which of the following is an important function of the power-up self-test?
    a. To determine the router hardware and software components and list them on the console terminal
    b. To cause other instructions to be loaded into memory
    c. To execute diagnostics that verify the basic operation of router hardware
    d. To start routing processes, supply addresses for interfaces, and set up media characteristics

4. Which of the following is an important result of Cisco IOS loading onto a router?
    a. Determining the router hardware and software components, and listing them on the console terminal
    b. Causing other instructions to be loaded into memory
    c. Executing diagnostics that verify the basic operation of router hardware
    d. Starting routing processes, supplying addresses for interfaces, and setting up media characteristics

5. Which of the following is an important result of the configuration file loading onto a router?
    a. Determining the router hardware and software components and listing them on the console terminal
    b. Causing other instructions to be loaded into memory
    c. Executing diagnostics that verify the basic operation of router hardware
    d. Starting routing processes, supplying addresses for interfaces, and setting up media characteristics

6. Which of the following is *not* a function of the router system startup routine?
    a. Verifying the routing of protocol packets
    b. Testing of the basic operations of router hardware
    c. Causing other instructions to be loaded into memory
    d. Starting routing processes, supplying addresses for interfaces, and setting up media characteristics

7. What is the function of the **erase startup-config** command?
    a. It deletes the backup configuration file in NVRAM.
    b. It deletes the bootstrap image from Flash memory.
    c. It deletes the current IOS from NVRAM.
    d. It deletes the current running configuration from Flash memory.

8. What is the function of the **reload** command?
    a. It loads a backup configuration file from a TFTP server.
    b. It saves the new IOS to Flash memory.
    c. It reboots the router.
    d. It loads the new configuration file in NVRAM.

9. Which router command deletes the backup configuration file in NVRAM?
    a. **delete backup-config**
    b. **erase backup-config**
    c. **delete startup-config**
    d. **erase startup-config**

10. Which router command causes the router to reboot?
    a. **reload**
    b. **restart**
    c. **reboot**
    d. **rerun**

11. When is the router setup mode executed?
    a. After the saved configuration file is loaded into main memory
    b. When the network administrator needs to enter complex protocol features on the router
    c. When the router begins software initialization
    d. When the router cannot find a valid configuration file

12. Which of the following does *not* describe features of the router setup mode?
    a. Many default settings appear in square brackets.
    b. The prompt and command for the setup mode are "router# setup".
    c. The first line and title of the setup dialog is "System Configuration Dialog".
    d. Pressing the Return key cancels dialog prompts.

13. Which of the following correctly describes a procedure for setup of router global and interface parameters on a router?
    a. A default parameter is shown in square brackets at every prompt.
    b. The router hostname must be set.
    c. An enable secret password can be set, but is not required.
    d. For each installed interface, a series of questions must be answered.

14. Which of the following does *not* correctly describe a procedure for setup of global and interface parameters on a router?
    a. An enable secret password must be entered.
    b. A default parameter is shown in square brackets at every prompt.
    c. Configuration values that you have determined for the installed interfaces are entered as parameters at the interface prompts.
    d. The router hostname must be set.

15. What information do you need to gather before starting a global or interface configuration session on a router?
    a. Brand and model of router and type of networks the router connects to directly.
    b. IOS version and current register setting.
    c. Which routing protocols will be needed, IP addresses of interface and subnets, and which interfaces are being used.
    d. IP addresses of neighboring routers, size of Flash memory.

16. Which of the following correctly describes the router setup script review?
    a. The setup command program displays the configuration that was created from your answers to the setup prompts.
    b. The setup command program asks you if you want to change any of your answers.
    c. If you choose to use the displayed configuration, you select a location to save it to.
    d. If you choose not to use the configuration, you must reboot the router.

17. Which of the following correctly describes the procedure for modifying the script displayed upon completion of the router configuration process?
    a. The setup command program prompts you at each of the script lines as to whether you want to change your answers.
    b. You choose not to accept the configuration and the router then reboots.
    c. You select the dialog lines that you want to change and the program then prompts you again at those lines.
    d. The script tells you to use configuration mode to modify the configuration.

18 Why might you want to issue **show startup-config** and **show running-config** commands?
   a. It's time to update the IOS and you need to kill certain router processes before proceeding.
   b. To determine the time since the router booted and the current register setting.
   c. The router suddenly isn't working right and you want to compare the initial state to the present state.
   d. To find out where the IOS booted from and which version is being used.

19. Why should the enable password be different than the enable secret password?
   a. The router asks that the passwords be changed monthly if they are the same
   b. To provide an additional category of users
   c. The enable password can be read directly from the configuration file
   d. The IOS behaves badly if they are the same

20. What file(s) would you find in NVRAM?
   a. IOS and configuration files
   b. Configuration file
   c. Backup copy of IOS
   d. Limited version IOS and registry files

Engineering Journal (Continued)

Chapter 20   Router Configuration 1

Introduction

The router uses information from the configuration file when it starts up. The configuration file contains commands to customize router operation. As you saw in the previous chapter, if no configuration file is available, the system configuration dialog setup guides you through creating one.

Concept Questions

Demonstrate your knowledge of these concepts by answering the following questions in the space provided.

Configuration files can come from the console, NVRAM, or a TFTP server. The router has several modes:

- Privileged mode is used for copying and managing entire configuration files.
- Global configuration mode is used for one-line commands and commands that change the entire router.
- Other configuration modes are used for multiple command lines and detailed configurations.

The router provides a hostname, a banner, and interface descriptions to aid in identification.

- **What does it mean to configure a router?**

- **Why must routers be configured?**

- **Explain how to work with 11.x config files, compare and contrast router configuration modes, and flowchart 11.x configuration methods.**

Engineering Journal
In the space provided, answer the Concept Questions.

_____
_____
_____
_____
_____
_____
_____
_____
_____
_____

Engineering Journal (Continued)

Vocabulary Exercise Chapter 20   **Name:** _____

Date: _____   **Class:** _____

Define the following term as completely as you can.

Configure terminal

_____
_____
_____

Focus Questions   **Name:** _____

Date: _____   **Class:** _____

1. What does it mean to configure a router? Why must routers be configured?

    _____

    _____

    _____

2. The commands **copy running-config tftp** and **copy running-config startup-config**
    store the currently running configuration from RAM to _____ and _____,
    respectively.

    _____

    _____

    _____

3. What do the prompts for user EXEC mode, privileged EXEC mode, and global
    configuration mode look like?

    _____

    _____

    _____

4. When configuring routers with Release 11.x methods, after you type **show running-
    config** and display a desired configuration, what commands do you use to save
    changes to backup?

    _____

    _____

    _____

5. What are two basic tasks when first configuring a router?

    _____

    _____

    _____

CCNA Exam Review Questions
The following questions help you prepare for the CCNA Exam. Answers are found in
Appendix A, "Answers to the CCNA Exam Review Questions."

1. Which of the following is *not* a function of the privileged EXEC **configure**
   command?
   a. To configure a router from a virtual terminal
   b. To configure a TFTP server from a virtual terminal
   c. To configure a router from the console terminal
   d. To load a configuration from a network TFTP server

2. Which of the following is *not* a step in using the **copy running-config tftp** command
   to store the current router configuration? (The steps are listed in order.)
   a. Enter the **copy running-config tftp** command.
   b. Enter the IP address of the router.
   c. Enter the name you want to assign to the configuration file.
   d. Confirm your choices.

3. Which of the following is *not* a step in using the **copy tftp running-config** command
   to load a router configuration file stored on a TFTP server? (The steps are listed in
   order.)
   a. Enter the **copy tftp running-config** command.
   b. Select either a host configuration file or a network configuration file.
   c. Enter the IP address of the remote host from which you retrieve the
      configuration file.
   d. Enter the name of the server to which you will load the file.

4. Which of the following does *not* correctly describe using a TFTP server to maintain
   router configuration files?
   a. A host configuration file contains commands that apply to all routers and
      terminal servers on the network.
   b. The convention for all filenames is UNIX-based.
   c. The default filename is **hostname-config** for the host file.
   d. Reconfiguration of the router occurs as soon as a new file is downloaded to
      the router.

5. You want to replace your current configuration file with one located on a TFTP
   server, what is the process you need to go through to do this?
   a. router (config)# **copy tftp running-config**
      Host or network configuration file [host]?
      IP address of remote host [255.255.255.255]? 131.108.6.155
      Name of configuration file [Router-config]? paris.3
      Configure using paris.3 from 131.108.6.155 [confirm] y
      Booting paris.3 from 131.108.6.155: !! [OK – 874/16000 bytes]
      Router (config)#

    b.   router # **copy tftp running-config**
        Host or network configuration file [host]?
        IP address of remote host [255.255.255.255]? 131.108.6.155
        Configure using paris.3 from 131.108.6.155 [confirm] y
        Booting paris.3 from 131.108.6.155: !! [OK – 874/16000 bytes]
        Router#

    c.   router # **copy tftp running-config**
        Host or network configuration file [host]?
        Name of configuration file [Router-config]? paris.3
        Configure using paris.3 from 131.108.6.155 [confirm] y
        Booting paris.3 from 131.108.6.155: !! [OK – 874/16000 bytes]
        Router#

    d.   router # **copy tftp running-config**
        Host or network configuration file [host]?
        IP address of remote host [255.255.255.255]? 131.108.6.155
        Name of configuration file [Router-config]? paris.3
        Configure using paris.3 from 131.108.6.155 [confirm] y
        Booting paris.3 from 131.108.6.155: !! [OK – 874/16000 bytes]
        Router#

6. What is the function of the **configure memory** router command?
    a. Loads configuration information from NVRAM
    b. Erases the contents of NVRAM
    c. Stores into NVRAM the current configuration in RAM
    d. Displays the configuration saved in NVRAM

7. What is the function of the **copy running-config startup-config** router command?
    a. Loads configuration information from NVRAM
    b. Erases the contents of NVRAM
    c. Stores into NVRAM the current configuration in RAM
    d. Displays the configuration saved in NVRAM

8. You added a new LAN onto you network; therefore, you updated your routing table and other parts of your configuration file. What command do you need to issue to save the new configuration file?
    a. **copy config startup-config**
    b. **copy running-config startup-config**
    c. **configure memory**
    d. **copy startup-config config-running**

9. Which router mode is a subset of the EXEC commands available at the privileged
    EXEC mode?
    a. Global configuration mode
    b. User EXEC mode
    c. Interface configuration mode
    d. Router configuration mode

10. What is the system prompt for the user EXEC router mode?
    a. Router>
    b. Router#
    c. Router(config)#
    d. User EXEC

11. What happens when you type *exit* at a router mode prompt?
    a. A configuration mode prompt appears.
    b. The router logs you off.
    c. The router backs out one mode level.
    d. A question prompt appears, requesting a network device location.

12. What does the router prompt look like when you are in global configuration mode?
    a. router#
    b. router (config-router)#
    c. router (config)#
    d. router-config#

13. If you want to back completely out of config mode, what must you enter?
    a. **exit**
    b. **no config-mode**
    c. **control e**
    d. **control z**

14. If you type Control-Z to get out of config mode, where do you end up?
    a. User EXEC mode
    b. Privileged EXEC mode
    c. Global-config mode
    d. Router mode

15. If you are planning to configure an interface, what prompt should be on the router?
    a. router (config)#
    b. router (config-in)#
    c. router (config-intf)#
    d. router (Config-if)#

16. Which of the following does *not* describe a procedure for using the router global configuration mode?
   a. You type **configure** to enter global configuration mode.
   b. You can specify the terminal, NVRAM, or a file on a server as the source of configuration commands.
   c. You can type commands to configure specific interfaces.
   d. You can type a command to reach a prompt for the interface configuration mode.

17. Which of the following is the system prompt for the global configuration mode?
   a. Router#
   b. Router(config)#
   c. Router(config-global)#
   d. Router(config-router)#

18. Which of the following does *not* describe a step in the procedure for using the router configuration mode?
   a. Enter a global router protocol command type at the global configuration prompt.
   b. The Router(config-router)# prompt indicates you are in router configuration mode.
   c. Defaults can be selected for all available command options.
   d. Finish using this mode with the command **exit**.

19. Which of the following does *not* describe a step in the procedure for using the interface configuration mode?
   a. Enter a global interface type and number command at the global configuration prompt.
   b. The Router(config-if)# prompt indicates you are in interface configuration mode.
   c. Interfaces can be turned on and off using commands in this mode.
   d. Interface types are enabled at subcommands in this mode.

20. Which of the following is a correct order for the process of configuring a router? (Assume you have already made router changes in configuration mode.)
   a. (1) Save changes to backup, (2) decide if changes are your intended results, (3) examine results, (4) examine backup file
   b. (1) Examine results, (2) decide if changes are your intended results, (3) save changes to backup, (4) examine backup file
   c. (1) Decide if changes are your intended results, (2) examine backup file, (3) save changes to backup, (4) examine results
   d. (1) Examine results, (2) save changes to backup, (3) decide if changes are your intended results, (4) examine backup file

21. Which of the following best describes the process of configuring a router?
    a. (1) Examine results, (2) make changes in configuration mode, (3) remove changes, (4) decide if changes are your intended results
    b. (1) Decide if changes are your intended results, (2) make changes in configuration mode, (3) examine results, (4) remove changes
    c. (1) Make changes in configuration mode, (2) decide if changes are your intended results, (3) examine results, (4) remove changes
    d. (1) Make changes in configuration mode, (2) examine results, (3) decide if changes are your intended results, (4) remove changes

22. Which of the following is a command that can be used to save router configuration changes to a backup?
    a. Router# copy running-config tftp
    b. Router# show running-config
    c. Router# config mem
    d. Router# copy tftp running-config

23. Which of the following is *not* a command to remove router configuration changes?
    a. Router(config)# **no ...**
    b. Router# **config mem**
    c. Router# **copy running-config startup-config**
    d. Router# **copy tftp running-config**

24. Which of the following correctly describes password configuration on routers?
    a. All passwords are established in the privileged EXEC mode.
    b. All passwords alter the password character string.
    c. A password can be established on all incoming Telnet sessions.
    d. The **enable** password command restricts access to user EXEC mode.

25. Which of the following does *not* describe password configuration on routers?
    a. Passwords can be established in every configuration mode.
    b. A password can be established on any console terminal.
    c. The **enable-secret** password uses an encryption process to alter the password character string.
    d. All password establishment begins in the global configuration mode.

26. When you are setting passwords for vty 0 4, what access point to the router are you setting a password for?
    a. Line consoles
    b. Telnet sessions
    c. Remote host router
    d. Virtual hosts

27. The password set up with the **enable-secret** command is to control direct access to what?
    a. User EXEC mode
    b. Configure Interface mode
    c. Privilege EXEC mode
    d. Global Config mode

28. Which of the following correctly describes procedures for confirming router identification?
    a. Routers should be named only after initial testing of the network.
    b. If no name is configured, the system automatically assigns the router a number.
    c. You name the router in global configuration mode.
    d. The login banner can be configured to display system error messages.

29. Which of the following does *not* describe procedures for confirming router identification?
    a. If no name is configured, the system default router name is "Router".
    b. Naming your router to be the host should be one of the first network configuration tasks.
    c. The login banner is configured in global configuration mode.
    d. You can configure a message-of-the-day banner to display on specified terminals.

30. You want to create a message to let people know a little something about the network when they log on—what command enables you to do this?
    a. **banner mesg**
    b. **banner motd**
    c. **daily mesg**
    d. **daily motd**

Chapter 21   IOS Images

Introduction

The default source for Cisco IOS software depends on the hardware platform, but most commonly, the router looks to the configuration commands saved in NVRAM. Cisco IOS software offers several alternatives. You can specify other sources where the router should look for software, or the router uses its own fall back sequence as necessary to load software.

Settings in the configuration register enable alternatives for where the router will bootstrap Cisco IOS software. You can specify enabled config-mode boot system commands to enter fallback sources for the router to use in sequence. Save these statements in NVRAM to use during the next startup with the command **copy running-config startup-config**. The router uses these commands as needed, in sequence, when it restarts. However, if NVRAM lacks boot system commands the router can use, the system has its own fall back alternatives. The router falls back and uses default Cisco IOS in Flash memory. If Flash memory is empty, the router tries its next TFTP alternative. The router uses the configuration register value to form a filename from which to boot a default system image stored on a network server.

Concept Questions

Demonstrate your knowledge of these concepts by answering the following questions in the space provided.

Routers boot Cisco IOS software from
- Flash
- TFTP server
- ROM (not full Cisco IOS)
- Multiple source options provide flexibility and fallback alternatives

- **Why does the router need an operating system?**

- **Why might there be different versions of router operating systems?**

- **Explain the process by which the router locates IOS.**

- **Explain the configuration register.**

- **Compare and contrast the boot options for obtaining IOS: from Flash memory, from the network, and from ROM.**

- 188 -

- Describe the show version command and all the information it tells you.

- Describe the processes for creating a software image backup, upgrading the image from a network, and loading a software image backup.

Engineering Journal
In the space provided, answer the Concept Questions.

Vocabulary Exercise Chapter 21   Name: _____

Date: _____   Class: _____

Define the following terms as completely as you can.

Acknowledgment number

_____
_____
_____

ARP

_____
_____
_____

Autonomous system

_____
_____
_____

Bandwidth

_____
_____
_____

Broadcast

_____
_____
_____

Checksum

_____
_____
_____

Configuration register

_____
_____
_____

Delay

_____
_____
_____

Destination port

_____
_____
_____

Distance-vector routing algorithm

_____
_____
_____

DNS

_____
_____
_____

Dynamic routing

_____
_____
_____

EEPROM

_____
_____
_____

Enhanced

_____
_____
_____

Flooding

_____
_____
_____

Flow control

_____
_____
_____

Handshake

_____

_____

_____

HLEN

_____

_____

_____

Host

_____

_____

_____

IGRP

_____

_____

_____

Link-state routing algorithm

_____

_____

_____

MTU

_____

_____

_____

Network

_____

_____

_____

OSPF

_____

_____

_____

Ping

_____

_____

_____

RARP

_____
_____
_____

Reliability

_____
_____
_____

RIP

_____
_____
_____

Sequence number

_____
_____
_____

Source port

_____
_____
_____

Static route

_____
_____
_____

Subnetwork

_____
_____
_____

TCP

_____
_____
_____

Telnet

_____
_____
_____

Trace

_____
_____
_____

UDP

_____
_____
_____

Window

_____
_____
_____

Window size

_____
_____
_____

Focus Questions   **Name:** _____

Date: _____   **Class:** _____

1. Why does the router need an operating system? Why might there be different versions of router operating systems?

   _____

   _____

   _____

2. Routers can boot Cisco IOS software from where?
   a. Flash memory
   b. A TFTP server
   c. Both a and b

3. The router cannot be configured to look elsewhere if the IOS software is not in Flash memory.
   a. True
   b. False

4. The configuration register is an *n*-bit register in NVRAM. What is the value of *n*?
   a. 8
   b. 16
   c. 32

5. What command would you use to check the configuration register setting?
   a. **configure terminal**
   b. **config-register**
   c. **show version**

6. What does the first E in EEPROM stand for?
   a. Erasable
   b. Electronically
   c. Enable

CCNA Exam Review Questions
The following questions help you review for the CCNA exam. Answers are found in Appendix A, "Answers to the CCNA Exam Review Questions."

1. Which of the following correctly describes a method for specifying how a router loads the Cisco IOS software?
   a. Designate fallback sources for the router to use in sequence from NVRAM
   b. Configure the Cisco IOS software image for the location where it will bootstrap
   c. Manually boot a default system image at a virtual terminal
   d. Manually boot a default system image at the network server

2. Which is the sequence used by the router for automatic fallback to locate Cisco IOS software?
   a. (1) Flash, (2) NVRAM, (3) TFTP server
   b. (1) NVRAM, (2) TFTP server, (3) Flash
   c. (1) NVRAM, (2) Flash (3), TFTP server
   d. (1) TFTP server, (2) Flash (3), NVRAM

3. Which of the following does *not* describe configuration register settings for Cisco IOS bootstrapping?
   a. The order in which the router looks for system bootstrap information depends on the boot field setting.
   b. You change the configuration register setting with the command **config-register**.
   c. You use a hexadecimal number when setting the configuration register boot field.
   d. Use the **show running-config** command to check the boot field setting.

4. Which of the following is information displayed by the Cisco IOS **show version** command?
   a. Statistics about the router's memory
   b. Name of the system image
   c. Information about the Flash memory device
   d. Status of configured network protocols

5. Which command is used to discover the configuration register setting?
   a. **show register**
   b. **show running-config**
   c. **show version**
   d. **show startup-config**

6. Which of the following does *not* correctly describe a fallback option for booting Cisco IOS software?
   a. Flash memory provides storage that is not vulnerable to network failures.
   b. Loading Cisco IOS software from a TFTP server is a good option in case Flash memory becomes corrupted.
   c. The system image booted from ROM is usually a complete copy of Cisco IOS software.
   d. ROM might contain an older version of Cisco IOS software.

7. Which of the following correctly describes preparing to use a TFTP server to copy software to Flash memory?
   a. The TFTP server must be another router or a host system such as a UNIX workstation or a laptop computer.
   b. The TFTP host must be a system connected to an Ethernet network.
   c. The name of the router containing the Flash memory must be identified.
   d. The Flash memory must be enabled.

8. Which of the following is *not* a step in preparing to copy software from a TFTP host to Flash memory?
   a. Check the router to make sure you can see and write into Flash.
   b. Verify that the router has sufficient room to accommodate Cisco IOS software.
   c. Use the **show ip route** command to make sure you can access the TFTP server over the TCP/IP network.
   d. Check the TFTP server to make sure you know the file or file space for the Cisco IOS software image.

9. Which of the following does *not* describe the procedure to verify sufficient room in Flash memory for copying software?
   a. Use the **show flash** command.
   b. Identify the total memory in Flash, which is the available memory.
   c. Compare the available memory with the length of the Cisco IOS software image to be copied.
   d. If there is not enough available memory, you can try to obtain a smaller Cisco IOS software image.

10. How would you determine the size of the IOS image file on a TFTP server?
    a. Go to the Cisco Web site and consult the image file size table.
    b. Type **show version** on your router.
    c. Do **dir** or **ls** on the TFTP server.
    d. Telnet to the TFTP server and issue a **show files** command.

11. Which of the following is the fastest way to make sure the TFTP server is reachable prior to trying to transfer an IOS image file?
    a. Trace the TFTP server.
    b. Ping the TFTP server.
    c. Telnet to the TFTP server.
    d. Call the TFTP server administrator.

12. Why do you need to determine the file size of the IOS image on the TFTP server before transferring it to your router?
    a. To check that there is enough space in Flash to store the file
    b. To verify that the file is the correct IOS for your router
    c. To complete a trivial file transfer protocol operation, the file size must be known
    d. To calculate the download time for the file and thus, the amount of time the router will be out of service

13. What information is *not* provided in the Cisco image filename system?
    a. Capabilities of the image
    b. The platform on which the image runs
    c. Where the image runs
    d. Size of the image

14. Which of the following is *not* part of the procedure for creating a Cisco IOS software image backup to a TFTP server?
    a. Use the **show flash** command to learn the name of the system image file.
    b. Enter the **copy flash tftp** command to begin the copy process.
    c. Enter the IP address of the router holding the image file.
    d. You can rename the file during transfer.

15. Why does an administrator create a Cisco IOS software image backup?
    a. To verify that the copy in Flash is the same as the copy in ROM
    b. To provide a fallback copy of the current image prior to copying the image to a new router
    c. To create a fallback copy of the current image as part of procedures during recovery from system failure
    d. To create a fallback copy of the current image prior to updating with a new version

16. Which of the following is *not* part of the procedure for loading a new Cisco IOS software image to Flash memory from a TFTP server? (The procedures are listed in correct order.)
    a. Backup a copy of the current software image to the TFTP server.
    b. Enter the **copy flash tftp** command to download the new image from the server.
    c. The procedure asks if you are willing to erase Flash.
    d. A series of Vs on the display indicates successful check run verification.

17. Which of the following is *not* part of the procedure for loading a backup Cisco IOS software image to Flash memory from a TFTP server? (The procedures are listed in correct order.)
    a. Enter the **copy tftp flash** command.
    b. A prompt asks you for the IP address of the TFTP server.
    c. If a file with the same name exists in Flash memory, the file being copied automatically replaces it.
    d. Enter the **reload** command to boot up the router using the newly copied image.

18. What is the initial boot attempt if the router register is set to 0x2100?
    a. ROM Monitor
    b. TFTP server
    c. ROM
    d. Flash

19. What is the initial boot attempt if the router register is set to 0x2101?
    a. ROM Monitor
    b. TFTP server
    c. ROM
    d. Flash

20. What is the initial boot attempt if the router register is set to 0x2102?
    a. ROM Monitor
    b. TFTP server
    c. ROM
    d. Flash

Chapter 22   Router Configuration 2

Introduction
One way to begin understanding the way the Internet works is to configure a router. It is also one of the primary topics on the CCNA exam, and one of the most important and sought after skills of employers. Routers are complex devices that can have a wide variety of possible configurations.

Concept Questions

- **What does it mean to configure a router?**

- **Why must routers be configured?**

- **Describe the router configuration process.**

- **Explain the router password recovery procedure on 1600 and 2500 series routers.**

Engineering Journal
In the space provided, answer the Concept Questions.

_____
_____
_____
_____
_____
_____
_____
_____
_____
_____
_____
_____
_____
_____
_____
_____
_____
_____
_____
_____
_____

Engineering Journal (Continued)

CCNA Exam Review Questions

The following questions help you prepare for the CCNA Exam. Answers are found in Appendix A, "Answers to the CCNA Exam Review Questions."

1. What are the major elements of a typical router configuration?
    a. passwords; interfaces; routing protocols; DNS
    b. boot sequence; interfaces; tftp server; NVRAM
    c. NVRAM; ROM; DRAM; interfaces
    d. Interfaces; routing protocols; configuration register; flash

2. In a password recovery procedure, immediately after issuing a CNTRL-BREAK upon router startup, what should be the config register setting?
    a. 0x2102
    b. 0x2142
    c. 0x0000
    d. 0x10F

3. In a password recovery procedure, just before saving the running config and after you enable a new secret password, what should be the config register setting?
    a. 0x2102
    b. 0x2142
    c. 0x0000
    d. 0x10F

4. What is the correct syntax to enable rip on router A in the lab topology?
    a.
```
config t
router rip
int e0
ip address 192.5.5.1 255.255.255.0
no shutdown
description this is the first Ethernet Interface
CNTRL/Z
copy run start
```

    b.
```
config t
router rip
network 192.5.5.0
network 205.7.5.0
network 201.100.11.0
CNTRL/Z
copy run start
```

c.
```
config t
router rip
ip host LAB-A 192.5.5.1 207.5.1 201.100.11.1
ip host LAB-B 201.100.11.2 219.17.100.1 199.6.13.1
ip host LAB-C 199.6.13.2 223.8.151.1 204.204.7.1
ip host LAB-D 204.204.7.2 210.93.105.1
ip host LAB-E 210.93.105.2
CNTRL/Z
copy run start
```

d. None of the above

5. What is the correct syntax for completely configuring Ethernet and Serial Interfaces?
a.
```
config t
int e0
ip host LAB-A 192.5.5.1 207.5.1 201.100.11.1
ip host LAB-B 201.100.11.2 219.17.100.1 199.6.13.1
ip host LAB-C 199.6.13.2 223.8.151.1 204.204.7.1
ip host LAB-D 204.204.7.2 210.93.105.1
ip host LAB-E 210.93.105.2
CNTRL/Z
copy run start
```

b.
```
config t
int e0
network 192.5.5.0
network 205.7.5.0
network 201.100.11.0
CNTRL/Z
copy run start
```

c.
```
config t
int e0
ip address 192.5.5.1 255.255.255.0
no shutdown
description this is the first Ethernet Interface
CNTRL/Z
copy run start
```

d. None of the above

Chapter 23   TCP/IP

Introduction

The Transmission Control Protocol/Internet Protocol (TCP/IP) suite of protocols was developed as part of the research done by the Defense Advanced Research Projects Agency (DARPA). Later, TCP/IP was included with the Berkeley Software Distribution of UNIX.

The Internet protocols can be used to communicate across any set of interconnected networks. They are equally well suited for both LAN and WAN communication.

The Internet Protocol suite includes not only Layer 3 and Layer 4 specifications (such as IP and TCP), but also specifications for such common applications as e-mail, remote login, terminal emulation, and file transfer.

Concept Questions

Demonstrate your knowledge of these concepts by answering the following questions in the space provided.

The TCP/IP protocol stack has the following components:
- Protocols to support file transfer, e-mail, remote login, and other applications.
- Reliable and unreliable transports.
- Connectionless datagram delivery at the network layer ICMP provides control and message functions at the network layer.

- The TCP/IP protocol stack maps closely to the lower layers of the OSI reference model. **What function do the application protocols perform?**

- The transport layer performs two functions. **What are they?**

- **What kind of protocol is TCP?**

Engineering Journal
In the space provided, answer the Concept Questions.

_____
_____
_____
_____
_____
_____
_____
_____

Engineering Journal (Continued)

Vocabulary Exercise Chapter 23   Name: _____

Date: _____   Class: _____

Define the following terms as completely as you can.

Acknowledgment number

_____
_____
_____

ARP

_____
_____
_____

Checksum

_____
_____
_____

Destination port

_____
_____
_____

Flow control

_____
_____
_____

Handshake

_____
_____
_____

HLEN

_____
_____
_____

RARP

_____
_____
_____

Sequence number

_____
_____
_____

Source port

_____
_____
_____

TCP

_____
_____
_____

UDP

_____
_____
_____

Window

_____
_____
_____

Window size

_____
_____
_____

Focus Questions   **Name:** _____

Date: _____   **Class:** _____

1. How do the TCP/IP conceptual layers relate to the OSI layers?

    _____

    _____

    _____

2. Compare and contrast TCP and UDP.

    _____

    _____

    _____

3. Briefly describe everything you know about the fields in a TCP segment.

    _____

    _____

    _____

4. Briefly describe everything you know about the fields in an IP datagram.

    _____

    _____

    _____

5. Briefly distinguish between IP, ICMP, ARP, and RARP.

    _____

    _____

    _____

CCNA Exam Review Questions

The following questions help you prepare for the CCNA Exam. Answers are found in Appendix A, "Answers to the CCNA Exam Review Questions."

1. Which of the following best describes TCP/IP?
    a. Suite of protocols that can be used to communicate across any set of interconnected networks
    b. Suite of protocols that allows LANs to connect into WANs
    c. Protocols that allow for data transmission across a multitude of networks
    d. Protocols that allow different devices to be shared by interconnected networks

2. Which of the following best describes the purpose of TCP/IP protocol stacks?
    a. Maps closely to the OSI reference model in the upper layers
    b. Supports all standard physical and data-link protocols
    c. Transfers information in a sequence of datagrams
    d. Reassembles datagrams into complete messages at the receiving location

3. The function of the application layer of the TCP/IP conceptual layers is best described by which of the following?
    a. Responsible for breaking messages into segments and then reassembling them at the destination
    b. Acts as a protocol to manage networking applications
    c. Exists for file transfer, e-mail, remote login, and network management
    d. Resends anything that is not received, and reassembles messages from the segments

4. Why are TCP three-way handshake/open connections used?
    a. To ensure that lost data can be recovered if problems occur later
    b. To determine how much data the receiving station can accept at one time
    c. To provide more efficient use of bandwidth by users
    d. To change binary ping responses into information in the upper layers

5. What does a TCP sliding window do?
    a. It makes the window larger so more data can come through at once, which results in more efficient use of bandwidth.
    b. The window size slides to each section of the datagram to receive data, which results in more efficient use of bandwidth.
    c. It allows the window size to be negotiated dynamically during the TCP session, which results in more efficient use of bandwidth.
    d. It limits the incoming data so that each segment must be sent one by one, which is an inefficient use of bandwidth.

6. What do the TCP sequence and acknowledgment numbers do?
   a. They break datagrams into their binary coefficients, number them sequentially, and send them to their destination, where the sender acknowledges their receipt.
   b. They break messages down into datagrams that are numbered and then sent to a host according to the sequence set by the source TCP.
   c. They provide a system for sequencing datagrams at the source and acknowledging them at the destination.
   d. They provide sequencing of segments with a forward reference acknowledgment, number datagrams before transmission, and reassemble the segments into a complete message.

7. Why does UDP use application layer protocols to provide reliability?
   a. To speed up transmission over the network.
   b. The lack of reliability protocols makes the software less expensive and easier to configure.
   c. It lacks a protocol to sequence datagrams and negotiate window size.
   d. It does not use windowing or acknowledgements.

8. What does the acronym ICMP stand for?
   a. Internetwork Connection Model Protocol
   b. Internet Connection Monitor Protocol
   c. Internet Control Message Protocol
   d. Internetwork Control Mode Protocol

9. What is the purpose of ICMPs?
   a. They put the internetwork in control mode so that protocols can be set up.
   b. They are messages that the network uses to monitor connection protocols.
   c. They are standard binary messages that act as model internetwork protocols.
   d. They are messages carried in IP datagrams used to send error and control messages.

10. What does the acronym ARP stand for?
    a. Address Resource Protocol
    b. Address Resolution Protocol
    c. Address Research Program
    d. Address Routing Program

11. What is the function of ARP?
    a. It completes research for a destination address for a datagram.
    b. It is used to develop a cached address resource table.
    c. It is used to map an IP address to a MAC address.
    d. It sends a broadcast message looking for the router address.

12. How does a sender find out the destination's MAC address?
    a. It consults its routing table.
    b. It sends a message to all the addresses searching for the address.
    c. It sends out a broadcast message to the entire LAN.
    d. It sends out a broadcast message to the entire network.

13. What is the function of the RARP?
    a. It is a protocol in the TCP/IP stack that provides a method for finding IP addresses based on MAC addresses.
    b. It is a protocol used to map a 32-bit IP address to a MAC address.
    c. It is a protocol used to develop a cached address resource table for the router.
    d. It a protocol that completes research for a destination address for a datagram based on the IP address.

14. Which of the following best describes the purpose of checksum?
    a. Method for comparing IP addresses against those permitted access to allow entry by a host
    b. Method for checking the integrity of transmitted data.
    c. Method for computing a sequence of octets taken through a series of arithmetic operations.
    d. Method for recomputing IP address values at the receiving end and comparing them for verification.

15. Which of the following best describes flow control?
    a. A device at the destination side that controls the flow of incoming data
    b. A buffer at the source side that monitors the outflow of data
    c. A technique that ensures that the source does not overwhelm the destination with data
    d. A suspension of transmission until the data in the source buffers has been processed

16. What does the acronym SNMP stand for?
    a. Standard Node Monitor Protocol
    b. Standard Network Management Protocol
    c. Simple Node Management Protocol
    d. Simple Network Management Protocol

17. What is the purpose of SNMP?
    a. Means to monitor and control network devices and to manage configurations, statistics collection, performance, and security
    b. Means to monitor the devices that are connected to one router, and assign a regular address to each host on the node network
    c. Protocol that provides the network administrator with the ability to manage the devices on the network and control who has access to each node
    d. Protocol that allows for the management of network security, performance, and configuration from a remote host

18. Which of the following best describes TTL?
    a. Field in the datagram header that determines how long the data is valid
    b. Field in an IP header that indicates how long a packet is considered valid
    c. Field within an IP datagram that indicates the upper-layer protocol sending the datagram
    d. Field in a datagram head that indicates when the next data packet will arrive

19. Which of the following best describes UDP?
    a. A protocol that acknowledges flawed or intact datagrams
    b. A protocol that detects errors and requests retransmissions from the source
    c. A protocol that processes datagrams and requests retransmissions when necessary
    d. A protocol that exchanges datagrams without acknowledgments or guaranteed delivery

20. Which of the following best describes window size?
    a. The maximum size of the window that a software can have and still process data rapidly
    b. The number of messages that can be transmitted while awaiting an acknowledgment
    c. The size of the window, in picas, that must be set ahead of time so data can be sent
    d. The size of the window opening on a monitor, which is not always equal to the monitor size

Chapter 24   IP Addressing

Introduction

In a TCP/IP environment, end stations communicate with servers or other end stations. This occurs because each node using the TCP/IP protocol suite has a unique 32-bit logical address. This address is known as the *IP address*.

Each company listed on the internetwork is seen as a single unique network that must be reached before an individual host within that company can be contacted. Each company network has an address; the hosts that live on that network share that same network address, but each host is identified by the unique host address on the network.

Concept Questions

Demonstrate your knowledge of these concepts by answering the following questions in the space provided.

- IP addresses are specified in 32-bit dotted decimal format. **Explain how to develop an IP address.**

- Router interfaces can be configured with an IP address.

- **ping** and **trace** commands can be used to verify IP address configuration. **What actually happens when you issue a ping command? Explain verbally and with a sketch.**

Engineering Journal
In the space provided, answer the Concept Questions.

_____
_____
_____
_____
_____
_____
_____
_____
_____
_____
_____
_____
_____
_____

Engineering Journal (Continued)

Vocabulary Exercise Chapter 24   **Name:** _____

Date: _____   **Class:** _____

Define the following terms as completely as you can.

Broadcast

_____
_____
_____

DNS

_____
_____
_____

Flooding

_____
_____
_____

Host

_____
_____
_____

Network

_____
_____
_____

Ping

_____
_____
_____

Subnetwork

_____
_____
_____

Telnet

_____
_____
_____

Trace

Focus Questions   **Name:** _____

Date: _____   **Class:** _____

1. If a router has a serial interface S0 with IP address 172.16.1.2, an Ethernet interface E0 with IP address 172.31.4.1, and a Token Ring interface T0 with an IP address of 172.31.16.1, and if all interfaces use a mask of 255.255.255.0, find the subnet (wire) number for each interface.

   _____
   _____
   _____

2. What is the result of the command Router (config-if)# **ip address ip-address subnet-mask**?

   _____
   _____
   _____

3. What does the **ip host** command do?

   _____
   _____
   _____

4. What type of information is obtained from the **show hosts** command?

   _____
   _____
   _____

5. Distinguish amongst the three commands that allow you to verify address configuration in your internetwork.

   _____
   _____
   _____

CCNA Exam Review Questions
The following questions help you prepare for the CCNA Exam. Answers are found in Appendix A, "Answers to the CCNA Exam Review Questions."

1. How does a router gain access to IP addresses?
    a. All host addresses must be entered individually by the network administrator.
    b. The router learns addresses from other routers.
    c. The network administrator creates a routing table of all addresses.
    d. All hosts automatically send their address to any available router.

2. What kind of address can a device or interface have?
    a. Any kind
    b. A network number and then all ones
    c. A nonzero network number
    d. A nonzero host number

3. If a router has an Ethernet interface E0, with IP address 172.31.4.1, and if the interface uses a mask of 255.255.255.0, what is the subnet number?
    a. E0: 172.16.1.0
    b. E0: 172.31.4.0
    c. E0: 172.31.16.0
    d. E0: 172.31.41.0

4. If you wanted to assign an address and a subnet mask and start IP processing on an interface, what command would you use?
    a. IP address subnet mask
    b. IP address
    c. Subnet mask
    d. Address IP process

5. If you want to connect a name to an IP address, such as asu 129.219.0.0, what command structure would you use?
    a. IP host asu 129.219.0.0
    b. IP name asu 129.219.0.0
    c. IP host name asu 129.219.0.0
    d. IP host address asu 129.219.0.0

6. What is the purpose of "tcp-port-number" in the ip host commands?
    a. It identifies which IP address to use when using the host name with an EXEC connect or Telnet command.
    b. It sets the default port of any device to port23.
    c. It sets the port of the source device in the router table.
    d. It identifies which TCP port to use when using the host name with an EXEC connect or Telnet command.

7. What is the purpose of the **ip name-server** command?
   a. It defines which hosts can provide the name service.
   b. It defines a naming scheme that allows a device to be identified by its location.
   c. It identifies which TCP port to use when using the host name.
   d. It generates messages from each router used along a datagram's path.

8. Which of the following best describes the function of the **show hosts** command?
   a. It identifies the subnet mask being used at the destination site.
   b. It maintains a cache of host name-to-address mappings for use by EXEC commands.
   c. It is used to display a cached list of host names and addresses.
   d. It shows the host name for the IP address.

9. When you use the **ping** command and get a result of "!," what does it mean?
   a. Successful receipt of an echo reply
   b. Times out waiting for datagram reply
   c. Destination unreachable error
   d. Congestion-experienced packet

10. What does it mean when you use the **ping** command and get a result of "." ?
    a. Successful receipt of an echo reply
    b. Timed out waiting for datagram reply
    c. Destination unreachable error
    d. Congestion-experienced packet

11. When you use the **ping** command and get a result of "U," what does it mean?
    a. Timed out waiting for datagram reply
    b. Destination unreachable error
    c. Congestion-experienced packet
    d. Ping interrupted

12. When you use the **ping** command and get a result of "C," what does it mean?
    a. Packet Time-To-Live exceeded
    b. Ping interrupted
    c. Destination unreachable error
    d. Congestion-experienced packet

13. When you use the **ping** command and get a result of "I," what does it mean?
    a. Destination unreachable error
    b. Ping interrupted
    c. Congestion-experienced packet
    d. Packet type unknown

14. When you use the **ping** command and get a result of "?," what does it mean?
    a. Packet Time-To-Live exceeded
    b. Ping interrupted
    c. Packet type unknown
    d. Congestion-experienced packet

15. When you use the **ping** command and get a result of "&," what does it mean?
    a. Congestion-experienced packet
    b. Ping interrupted
    c. Packet type unknown
    d. Packet Time-To-Live exceeded

16. Which of the following best describes the function of the extended command mode of the **ping** command?
    a. Used to specify the supported Internet header options
    b. Used to specify the time frame for the ping return
    c. Used to diagnose why aping was delayed or not returned
    d. Used to trace the datagram as it passes through each router

17. How do you enter the extended mode of the **ping** command?
    a. **ping x**
    b. **ping e**
    c. **ping** [return key]
    d. **ping m**

18. What does the response "!H" mean, when it comes in response to the **trace** command?
    a. The probe was received by the router, but was not forwarded.
    b. The protocol was unreachable and the trace was terminated.
    c. The network was unreachable, but the last router was up.
    d. The port was reached, but the wire to the network was malfunctioning.

19. When it comes in response to the **trace** command, what does the response "P" mean?
    a. Time out.
    b. The port was unreachable.
    c. The protocol was unreachable.
    d. The network was unreachable.

20. What does the response "N" mean, when it comes in response to the **trace** command?
    a. The name has no IP address connected to it.
    b. The probe was not received, so it could not be forwarded.
    c. The protocol was unreachable.
    d. The network was unreachable.

21. When it comes in response to the **trace** command, what does the response "U" mean?
    a. The address was unreachable.
    b. The protocol was unreachable.
    c. The network was unreachable.
    d. The port was unreachable.

22. What does the response "*" mean when it comes in response to the **trace** command?
    a. The destination device refused the trace.
    b. The trace timed out.
    c. The network refused the trace.
    d. The source used a trace that was not supported by the network protocol.

Chapter 25   Routing

Introduction

Which path should traffic take through the cloud of networks? Path determination occurs at Layer 3 of the OSI reference model, the network layer. The path determination function enables a router to evaluate the available paths to a destination and to establish the preferred handling of a packet.

Routing services use network topology information when evaluating network paths. This information can be configured by the network administrator or collected through dynamic processes running in the network.

The network layer interfaces to networks and provides best-effort, end-to-end packet delivery services to its user, the transport layer. The network layer sends packets from the source network to the destination network based on the IP routing table.

After the router determines which path to use, it proceeds with forwarding the packet: It takes the packet it accepted on one interface and forwards it to another interface or port that reflects the best path to the packet's destination.

Concept Questions

Demonstrate you knowledge of these concepts by answering the following questions in the space provided.

- Internetworking functions of the network layer include network addressing and best path selection for traffic. **What is best path selection?**

- In network addressing, one part of the address is used to identify the path used by the router and the other is used for ports or devices on the network. **Which part of the address is used to identify the path used by the router?**

- Routed protocols allow routers to direct user traffic, and routing protocols work between routers to maintain path tables. **Explain this key difference.**

- Network discovery for distance-vector routing involves exchange of routing tables; problems can include slow convergence. **What other problems can occur as a result of exchanging routing tables?**

- For link-state routing, routers calculate the shortest paths to other routers; problems can include inconsistent updates. **What other problems might occur with link-state routing?**

- Balanced hybrid routing uses attributes of both link-state and distance-vector routing, and can apply paths to several protocols. **What advantages does balance hybrid routing offer?**

Engineering Journal
In the space provided, answer the Concept Questions.

_____

_____

_____

_____

_____

_____

_____

_____

_____

_____

_____

_____

_____

_____

_____

_____

_____

_____

_____

_____

_____

_____

_____

_____

_____

_____

_____

_____

_____

_____

_____

_____

_____

_____

_____

_____

_____

Vocabulary Exercise Chapter 25   **Name:** _____

Date: _____   **Class:** _____

Define the following terms as completely as you can.

Default route

_____
_____
_____

Delay

_____
_____
_____

Dynamic routing

_____
_____
_____

Enhanced IGRP

_____
_____
_____

Header

_____
_____
_____

Hop count

_____
_____
_____

Hop

_____
_____
_____

IGRP

_____
_____
_____

OSPF

_____
_____
_____

RIP

_____
_____
_____

Routing metric

_____
_____
_____

Routing protocol

_____
_____
_____

Static route

_____
_____
_____

Stub network

_____
_____
_____

Focus Questions   Name: _____

Date: _____   Class: _____

1. What does a router do? What improvements do network addresses offer over physical addresses?

    _____

    _____

    _____

2. Distinguish between routed protocols and routing protocols.

    _____

    _____

    _____

    _____

    _____

    _____

3. How does multiprotocol routing enable the Internet to exist?

    _____

    _____

    _____

    _____

    _____

    _____

4. List and briefly describe at least five examples of routing metrics.
    The metrics most commonly used by routers include the following:
        Bandwidth
        Delay
        Load
        Reliability
        Hop count
        Ticks
        Cost

    _____

    _____

    _____

    _____

    _____

    _____

    _____

    _____

    _____

5. Briefly describe distance-vector routing.

_____
_____
_____
_____
_____
_____

CCNA Exam Review Questions

The following questions help review for the CCNA exam. Answers are found in Appendix A, "Answers to the CCNA Exam Review Questions."

1. What function allows routers to evaluate available routes to a destination and to establish the preferred handling of a packet?
   a. Data linkage
   b. Path determination
   c. SDLC interface protocol
   d. Frame Relay

2. What information is used by routing services to evaluate network paths?
   a. MAC addresses
   b. Name server tables
   c. Network topology
   d. ARP requests

3. Where can routing services obtain the network topology information needed to evaluate network paths?
   a. From RARP and ARP tables
   b. From network name servers
   c. From bridges talking to routers during messaging sessions
   d. From information collected by dynamic processes

4. What two functions do a router use to relay packets from one data link to another?
   a. Link-state testing and convergence
   b. Convergence and switching
   c. Path determination and link-state testing
   d. Path determination and switching

5. How does the network layer send packets from the source to the destination?
   a. Uses an IP routing table
   b. Uses ARP responses
   c. Refers to a name server
   d. Refers to the bridge

6. What happens at the router during a switching operation?
   a. The router changes from link-state to distance-vector mode.
   b. A packet accepted on one interface is forwarded to another interface or port that reflects the best path to the destination.
   c. A test message is sent over the proposed route to make sure it is operational.
   d. The received packet has the header stripped, read, and a new header attached listing the next stop on the route.

7. Why is it important to prevent unnecessary broadcasts over the entire internetwork?
   a. Broadcasts incur processing overhead and waste network capacity.
   b. Broadcasts cannot be sent as multiphase transmissions so routers must change modes to deal with them.
   c. Broadcasts are common causes of collisions and should be avoided whenever possible.
   d. Broadcasts can quickly relay bad routing tables throughout an internetwork.

8. How does the network layer avoid unnecessary broadcast messages?
   a. By using error-trapping algorithms
   b. By using consistent end-to-end addressing
   c. By using name servers to do look-up functions
   d. By using link-state detection

9. What problem for the network layer does using consistent end-to-end addressing solve?
   a. Reduces chance of infinite loops
   b. Avoids split horizons
   c. Avoids unnecessary broadcast messages
   d. Reduces count to infinity problems

10. What are the two parts of an address that routers use to forward traffic through a network?
    a. Network address and host address
    b. Network address and MAC address
    c. Host address and MAC address
    d. MAC address and subnet mask

11. Which network device uses the network address to define a path?
    a. Bridge
    b. Router
    c. Hub
    d. Server

12. How does a router make path selections?
    a. By looking at the network portion of the address
    b. By looking at the host portion of the address
    c. By looking at mean distances between routers
    d. By looking at the port or device on the network

13. What does the host address specify?
    a. Type of device
    b. Distance to the nearest network hub
    c. Specific port or device on the network
    d. Network the device is on

14. How does the host portion of an address help a router in its path determination function?
    a. Defines a path through the network
    b. Contains distance information that can be used to calculate the shortest route
    c. Refers to a specific port on the router that leads to an adjacent router in that direction
    d. Tells the router the type of device and its distance from the router

15. What does the switching function of a router do?
    a. Allows greater throughput and capacity by multitasking
    b. Allows the router to accept a packet on one interface and forward it on another interface
    c. Exchanges the old header of a data packet for a new header that includes path information for the next router
    d. Changes the router from receive and send mode to broadcast mode when part of the network fails

16. Which best describes a routed protocol?
    a. Provides enough information to allow a packet to be forwarded from host to host
    b. Provides information necessary to pass data packets up to the next highest network layer
    c. Allows routers to communicate with other routers to maintain and update address tables
    d. Allows routers to bind MAC and IP address together

17. Which is an example of a routed protocol?
    a. RIP
    b. IP
    c. IGRP
    d. OSPF

18. Which best describes a routed protocol?
    a. Passes data packets up to the next highest network layer
    b. Binds MAC and IP addresses together
    c. Defines the format and use of fields within a packet
    d. Exchanges routing tables and shares routing information between routers

19. Which best describes a routing protocol?
    a. Provides information to allow a packet to be forwarded from host to host
    b. Binds MAC and IP addresses together
    c. Defines the format and use of fields within a data packet
    d. Allows routers to communicate with other routers to maintain and update address tables

20. Which best describes a routing protocol?
    a. A protocol that accomplishes routing through the implementation of an algorithm
    b. A protocol that specifies how and when MAC and IP addresses are bound together
    c. A protocol that defines the format and use of fields within a data packet
    d. A protocol that allows a packet to be forwarded from host to host

21. Which best describes the difference between a routed versus a routing protocol?
    a. Routed protocols are used between routers to maintain tables, while routing protocols are used between routers to direct traffic.
    b. Routed protocols use distance-vector algorithms, while routing protocols use link-state algorithms.
    c. Routed protocols are used between routers to direct traffic, while routing protocols used between routers to maintain tables.
    d. Routed protocols use dynamic addressing, while routing protocols use static addressing.

22. What happens when a data-link frame is received on a router interface?
    a. The packet header is removed and a new one with additional routing information is attached.
    b. A frame header is sent to check the path integrity prior to sending the packet on towards its destination.
    c. The packet is sent to the nearest bridge that forwards it to the next router or the final destination.
    d. The header is examined to determine the destination network and consults the routing table to see which outgoing interface is associated with that network.

23. What happens after a router has matched the destination network with an outgoing interface?
    a. The packet is sent to the nearest bridge that forwards it to the next router or the final destination.
    b. A frame header is sent to check the path integrity prior to sending the packet on towards its destination.
    c. The packet is queued for delivery to the next hop in the path.
    d. The packet header is removed and a new one with additional routing information is attached.

24. Which of the following best describes a data-link frame header?
    a. Controls information placed in front of data when it is readied for network transmission
    b. Broadcasts message sent over the network to warn routers of network failures in specific links
    c. Diagnostic message used to check network links for problems
    d. Packets sent by routers to other routers to update routing tables

25. What is the control information placed in front of data in a data packet called?
    a. Addressing
    b. Header
    c. Trailer
    d. Encapsulate

26. Which of the following best describes a hop?
    a. Passage of a data packet between two routers
    b. Device which connects two or more networks together
    c. Shortest distance between source and destination
    d. Exchange and copying of ARP tables between two noncontiguous network devices

27. What is the passage of a data packet between two routers called?
    a. Exchange
    b. Hop
    c. Transmittal
    d. Signaling

28. Which best describes multiprotocol routing?
    a. Ability to send packets simultaneously out different ports
    b. Ability to shift from static to dynamic routing as network loads change
    c. Ability to maintain routing tables for several routed protocols concurrently
    d. Ability to rewrite frame headers to formats compatible with different networks

29. What does multiprotocol routing allow routers to do?
    a. Rewrite frame headers to formats compatible with different networks
    b. Shift from static to dynamic routing as network loads change
    c. Send packets simultaneously out different ports
    d. Deliver packets from several routed protocols over the same data links

30. Which best describes static routing?
    a. A route that is manually entered into a routing table by the network administrator
    b. A route received from the local name server
    c. A route that is automatically entered into a routing table
    d. An optimum route between devices as determined by the RARP table

31. Which best describes dynamic routing?
    a. Automatic updating of routing tables whenever new information is received from the internetwork
    b. Manual entry of data into a routing table by the network administrator
    c. Following preset paths from device to device
    d. RARP server determines optimum route between devices and copies those routes into a routing table

32. What type of routing occurs without the intervention of a network administrator?
    a. Default
    b. Dynamic
    c. Progressive
    d. Static

33. What is one advantage of static routing?
    a. More secure as parts of an internetwork can be hidden
    b. Requires little active management by the network administrator
    c. Adjusts automatically to topology or traffic changes
    d. Can compensate for router failures by using alternate paths

34. What is one advantage for using static routing on a stub network?
    a. Compensates for route failures by using alternate paths
    b. Requires little active management by the network administrator
    c. Adjusts automatically to topology or traffic changes
    d. Avoids the network overhead required by dynamic routing

35. What are the two major classes of routing algorithms?
    a. Checksum and link-state
    b. Checksum and traffic load
    c. Distance-vector and traffic load
    d. Distance-vector and link-state

36. Which best describes a distance-vector protocol?
    a. Determines the direction and distance to any link in the internetwork
    b. Each router maintains a complex database of internetwork topology information
    c. Computationally rather complex
    d. Method of routing which prevents loops and minimizes counting to infinity

37. What do distance-vector algorithms require of routers?
    a. Default routes for major internetwork nodes in case of corrupted routing tables
    b. Send its entire routing table in each update to its neighbors
    c. Fast response times and ample memory
    d. Maintain a complex database of internetwork topology information

38. Why is it important in distance-vector algorithms for routers to send copies of their routing table to neighboring routers?
    a. To prevent error propagation
    b. To stop routing loops
    c. To enable split horizon mapping
    d. To communicate topology changes quickly

39. What is a major drawback of distance-vector algorithms?
    a. More network traffic
    b. Computationally difficult
    c. Prone to routing loops
    d. Cannot implement hold-down timers

40. What is one disadvantage of distance-vector algorithms?
    a. Routers do not know the exact topology of an internetwork, only distances between points
    b. More network traffic
    c. Computationally difficult
    d. Cannot implement hold-down timers

41. What is one advantage of distance-vector algorithms?
    a. Not likely to count to infinity
    b. Implements easily on very large networks
    c. Not prone to routing loops
    d. Computationally simpler

42. Which of the following best describes link-state algorithms?
    a. Recreate the exact topology of the entire internetwork
    b. Require minimal computations
    c. Determine distance and direction to any link on the internetwork
    d. Use little network overhead and reduces overall traffic

43. Which of the following best describes link-state algorithms?
    a. Use little network overhead and reduces overall traffic
    b. Each router broadcasts information about the network to all nodes on the network
    c. Determine distance and direction to any link on the internetwork
    d. Use little network overhead and reduces overall traffic

44. What is true about link-state routing algorithms?
    a. Require less network traffic than distance-vector algorithms
    b. Computationally rather simple
    c. Require less router memory and slower response times
    d. Maintain full knowledge of distant routers and how they interconnect

45. Which best describes convergence?
    a. When messages simultaneously reach a router and a collision occurs
    b. When several routers simultaneously route packets along the same path
    c. When all routers in an internetwork have the same knowledge of the structure and topology of the internetwork
    d. When several messages are being sent to the same destination

46. Which term is used to describe an internetwork state when all routers have the same knowledge of the structure and topology of the internetwork?
    a. Congruence
    b. Equivalence
    c. Correspondence
    d. Convergence

47. Why is fast convergence a desirable attribute of a routing protocol?
    a. Reduces time period over which routers make incorrect routing decisions
    b. Reduces network traffic
    c. Reduces routing loop time
    d. Reduces memory requirements of local routers

48. After a network topology change, what routing protocol characteristic reduces incorrect or wasteful routing decisions?
    a. Symmetry
    b. Convergence
    c. Equivalence
    d. Correspondence

49. What is a routing loop?
    a. A route to often requested destinations
    b. A network path that is circular and has no branches
    c. A packet that cycles repeatedly through a constant series of network nodes
    d. A process that routers go through when performing self-diagnostics

50. What is the process called where packets never reach their destination, but instead cycle repeatedly through the same series of network nodes?
    a. Split horizon
    b. End-to-end messaging
    c. Convergence
    d. Routing loop

51. Why do routing loops occur?
    a. Slow convergence after a modification to the internetwork.
    b. Split horizons are artificially created.
    c. Network segments fail catastrophically and take other network segments down in a cascade effect.
    d. Default routes were never established and initiated by the network administrator.

52. Why do routing loops occur?
    a. Split horizons are artificially created.
    b. A network device fails and that information is only slowly passed to all the routers in the internetwork.
    c. Default routes were never established and initiated by the network administrator.
    d. Network segments fail catastrophically and take other network segments down in a cascade effect.

53. Why does the problem of counting to infinity occur?
    a. Split horizon
    b. Noncongruence
    c. Slow convergence
    d. Router inequivalence

54. Which best describes the count to infinity problem?
    a. Routers continuously increment the hop count as a routing loop proceeds.
    b. Packets cycle repeatedly through a constant series of network nodes.
    c. During heavy traffic periods, freak collisions can occur and damage the packet headers.
    d. After a split horizon occurs, two sets of metrics exists for the same destination and neither matches that in the routing table.

55. How can the count to infinity problem be prevented?
    a. By forcing a routing loop
    b. By invoking a split horizon process
    c. By tracking network traffic levels and regulating flow
    d. By imposing an arbitrary hop-count limit

56. How can the count to infinity problem be solved?
    a. Initiate a routing loop
    b. Define infinity as some maximum number
    c. Switch from distance-vector to link-state mode
    d. Force a router convergence and reconciliation

57. What happens once the hop-count exceeds the maximum in a routing loop?
    a. The loop ends and the data packet is returned to the source for retransmission later.
    b. The default route is recalled and used.
    c. The network is considered unreachable and the loop ends.
    d. A count to infinity is initiated and a split horizon invoked.

58. How can the count to infinity problem be prevented?
    a. By using routing loops
    b. By using split horizon routing systems
    c. By increasing router memory
    d. By using hold-down timers

59. Which best describes hold-down timers?
    a. Timer that synchronizes the router table update process
    b. Time during which messages are held if network segment is temporarily unavailable
    c. Time allowed before intervention to halt routing loop
    d. Time during which routers will neither send nor receive updated routing tables

60. Why are hold-down timers useful?
    a. They flush bad information about a route from all routers in the network.
    b. They force all routers in a segment to synchronize switching operations.
    c. They reduce the amount of network traffic during high traffic periods.
    d. They provide a mechanism for bypassing failed sections of network.

61. When are routers placed in a hold-down state?
    a. When a routing loop occurs
    b. When a link in a route fails
    c. When a routing table becomes corrupted
    d. When convergence occurs too slowly

62. How does a hold-down timer work?
    a. By holding messages in routing loops for a given time period, the hold-down timer reduces network traffic at peak times.
    b. When the hop count exceeds a fixed value, the hold-down timer holds the message until a split horizon is established.
    c. When a router receives an update indicating that a network is now inaccessible, the router marks the route and starts a hold-down timer.
    d. When a count is started, a hold-down timer is started too, if after a given time period the count continues, the timer halts the process and returns control to the nearest router.

63. What are the major two link-state concerns?
    a. Split horizons and convergence
    b. Processing and memory requirements
    c. Routing loops and equivalence
    d. Table copying and counting to infinity

64. Which of the following best describes link-state advertisement (LSA)?
    a. Broadcast message in response to a convergence call
    b. Broadcast message relaying state of data links (up or down) to all routers
    c. Broadcast packet that contains information about neighbors and path costs
    d. Broadcast packet that is initiated by an active routing loop

65. What are LSAs used for?
    a. To halt routing loops
    b. To determine path metrics
    c. To broadcast convergence calls
    d. To maintain routing tables of receiving routers

66. What is the most complex and important aspect of link-state routing?
    a. Making sure all routers get all the necessary LSA packets
    b. Ensuring that convergence occurs rapidly
    c. Avoiding routing loops during initial start up
    d. Providing mechanisms for split horizons and count to infinity avoidance

67. What will happen if routers have different sets of LSAs?
    a. A check sum procedure is initiated and faulty routing tables repaired.
    b. Routes become unreachable because routers disagree about a link.
    c. A master comparison is forced and subsequent convergence on a single routing table occurs.
    d. A broadcast message is sent with the master copy of the routing table to all routers.

68. What is one problem with link-state updating?
    a. Easy to start a routing loop and subsequent count to infinity
    b. Routers can become unreachable because they don't have a complete picture of the internetwork
    c. In synchronizing large networks, it is difficult to tell which updates are correct
    d. If the master routing table is corrupted, the entire network will go down

69. What is one problem with link-state updating?
    a. Routers can become unreachable because they don't have a complete picture of the internetwork.
    b. Easy to start a routing loop and subsequent count to infinity.
    c. If the master routing table is corrupted, the entire network will go down.
    d. Order of router startup alters the topology learned.

70. Which of the following is correct?
    a. Distance-vector routing gets all topological data from the routing tables of their neighbors, while link-state routing develops a map of the network by accumulating LSAs.
    b. Distance-vector routing develops a map of the network, while link-state routing gets topological data from the routing tables of their neighbors.
    c. Distance-vector routing requires lots of bandwidth and network overhead, while link-state routing requires considerably less.
    d. Distance-vector routing has quick convergence time, while link-state routing has a slow convergence time and is therefore prone to routing loops.

71. Which of the following is correct?
    a. Distance-vector routing requires lots of bandwidth and network overhead, while link-state routing requires considerably less.
    b. Distance-vector routing determines the best path by adding to the metric value it receives, while link-state routing has the routers calculating their own shortest path to destinations.
    c. Distance-vector routing has quick convergence time, while link-state routing has a slow convergence time and is therefore prone to routing loops.
    d. Distance-vector routing has the routers calculate their own shortest path to destinations, while link-state routing determines the best path by adding to the metric value it receives from its neighbors.

72. Which of the following is correct?
    a. Distance-vector routing has a quick convergence time, while link-state routing has a slow convergence time and is therefore prone to routing loops.
    b. Distance-vector routing requires lots of bandwidth and network overhead, while link-state routing requires considerably less.
    c. Distance-vector routing updates for topology changes with periodic table updates, while link-state routing updates are triggered by topology changes.
    d. Distance-vector routing updates are triggered by topology changes, while link-state routing updates for topology changes with periodic scheduled table updates.

73. Which best describes hybrid routing?
    a. Uses distance vectors to determine best paths, but topology changes trigger routing table updates
    b. Uses distance-vector routing to determine best paths between topology during high traffic periods
    c. Uses topology to determine best paths but does frequent routing table updates
    d. Uses topology to determine best paths but uses distance vectors to circumvent inactive network links

Chapter 26   Routing Protocols

Introduction

After testing the hardware and loading Cisco IOS system image, the router finds and applies the configuration statements. These entries provide the router with details about router-specific attributes, protocol functions, and interface addresses.

However, if the router faces a beginning condition where the router is unable to locate a valid startup-config file, it enters an initial router configuration mode called the *setup mode*.

With the setup mode command facility, you can answer questions in the System Configuration Dialog. This facility prompts you for basic configuration information. The answers you enter enable the router to use a sufficient, but minimal, feature router configuration, which includes the following:

- An inventory of interfaces
- An opportunity to enter global parameters
- An opportunity to enter interface parameters
- A setup script review
- An opportunity to indicate whether you want the router to use this configuration

After you approve setup-mode entries, the router uses the entries as a running configuration. The router also stores the configuration in NVRAM as a new startup-config. You can start using the router. For additional protocol and interface changes, use the enable mode and enter the command **configure**.

Concept Questions

Demonstrate your knowledge of these concepts by answering the following questions in the space provided.

- Routers can be configured to use one or more IP routing protocols. **Identify and briefly explain the different IP routing protocols.**

- Two IP routing protocols are RIP and IGRP.
  Compare and contrast these two IP routing protocols.

Engineering Journal

In the space provided, answer the Concept Questions.

_____
_____
_____
_____
_____
_____
_____
_____
_____
_____
_____
_____
_____
_____
_____
_____
_____
_____
_____
_____
_____
_____
_____
_____
_____
_____
_____
_____
_____
_____
_____
_____
_____
_____
_____
_____
_____
_____
_____
_____

Vocabulary Exercise Chapter 26   Name: _____

Date: _____   **Class:** _____

Define the following terms as completely as you can.

Autonomous system

_____

_____

_____

Bandwidth

_____

_____

_____

Delay

_____

_____

_____

Distance-vector routing algorithm

_____

_____

_____

Dynamic routing

_____

_____

_____

Enhanced IGRP

_____

_____

_____

IGRP

_____

_____

_____

Link-state routing algorithm

_____

_____

_____

MTU

_____

_____

_____

OSPF

_____

_____

_____

Reliability

_____

_____

_____

RIP

_____

_____

_____

Static route

_____

_____

_____

Focus Questions   **Name:** _____

Date: _____   **Class:** _____

1. Default routes are manually defined by the system administrator as the route to take when no route to the destination is known. They are also known as which of the following answers?
   a. Dynamic routes
   b. Default subnet
   c. Default network

2. Default routes are configured by using the _____ command, while in the _____ prompt.
   a. **ip default route**; Router (config)#
   b. **ip default-network**; Router (config)#
   c. **ip default-route**; Router(config-if)#

3. Which of the following are used to communicate within a given autonomous system?
   a. Routing Information Protocols
   b. Exterior Routing Protocols
   c. Interior Routing Protocols

4. Routing protocols can be configured on a router while in which of the following modes?
   a. Router#
   b. Router(config)#
   c. Router(config-if)#

5. Which of the following protocols sends updated routing table information onto the network every 90 seconds?
   a. IGRP
   b. RIP
   c. Exterior Gateway Protocol (EGP)

CCNA Exam Review Questions
The following questions help you review for the CCNA exam. Answers are found in Appendix A, "Answers to the CCNA Exam Review Questions."

1. If you start the router and it cannot find Cisco IOS system image, what happens?
   a. The router will not operate.
   b. The router will request that you make the Cisco IOS available.
   c. You will have to manually set up the router in the setup mode.
   d. The router will ask you to install any router operating system.

2. What command do you use to access the setup mode?
   a. **define**
   b. **exec**
   c. **setup**
   d. **configure**

3. If you manually set up the router, what type of configuration will it have?
   a. It will be fully configured.
   b. It will be minimally configured.
   c. You will only be able to use it to install Cisco IOS.
   d. It will be configured in such a way that no changes can be made, except manually.

4. What kind of entries does a router initially refer to?
   a. Entries about networks or subnets that are directly connected
   b. Entries it has learned about from the Cisco IOS software
   c. Entries whose IP address and mask information are known
   d. Entries it has learned about from other routers

5. Which of the following best describes a static route?
   a. Routing table entry that is used to direct frames for which a next hop is not explicitly listed in the routing table
   b. Route that is explicitly configured and entered into the routing table and takes precedence over routes chosen by dynamic routing protocols
   c. Route that adjusts automatically to network topology or traffic changes
   d. Route that adjusts involuntarily to direct frames within a network topology

6. Which of the following best describes a dynamic routing?
   a. Routing that is explicitly configured and entered into the routing table
   b. Routing that is used to direct frames for which a next hop is not explicitly listed in the routing table
   c. Routing that adjusts automatically to network topology or traffic changes
   d. Routing that adjusts involuntarily to direct frames within a network topology

7. What do link-state algorithms require routers to do?
   a. Flood routing information about the state of its own links to all nodes on the internetwork
   b. Flood all its routing information to all nodes on the internetwork
   c. Send a complete picture of the topology of the entire network to all nodes on the network
   d. Base routing table on information provided by the every other router and send IP information to all nodes on the network

8. An administrative distance of 15 would indicate which of the following?
   a. The IP address is static.
   b. The IP address is dynamic.
   c. The routing information source is trustworthy.
   d. The routing information source is untrustworthy.

9. Why are routing updates not sent to a link if it is only defined by a static route?
   a. Because each node in the network already knows the route
   b. To conserve bandwidth
   c. To keep routing tables small
   d. To keep routing tables organized

10. In the following command, what does the last number stand for?
    router (config)# **ip route 2.0.0.0 255.0.0.0 1.0.0.2 5**
    a. The number of hops
    b. The number of routes to the destination
    c. The administrative distance
    d. The destinations reference number in the routing table

11. Why would you set the administrative distance really high?
    a. The network uses Enhanced IGRP.
    b. The dynamic address may be better.
    c. The network uses OSPF.
    d. The network uses only uses default network addresses.

12. If you just added a new LAN onto your network and you want to add the routes to the new devices to your routing table, what command structure would you use?
    a. router (config)> ip route 2.0.0.0 255.0.0.0 1.0.0.2 5
    b. router (config)# ip route 2.0.0.0 255.0.0.0 1.0.0.2 5
    c. router (config)# ip route 2.0.0.0 1.0.0.2 5
    d. router (config)# ip route 2.0.0.0 255.0.0.0 1.0.0.2

Chapter 27 Network Troubleshooting

Introduction
Troubleshooting tools that you might use for the software (IOS) include **ping**, **trace ip route**, **telnet**, and **show arp**.

Concept Questions

Demonstrate your knowledge of these concepts by answering the following questions in the space provided.

- **Describe typical Layer 1 errors.**

- **Describe typical Layer 2 errors.**

- **Describe typical Layer 3 errors.**

- **Describe some network troubleshooting strategies.**

Engineering Journal
In the space provided, answer the Concept Questions.

_____
_____
_____
_____
_____
_____
_____
_____
_____
_____
_____
_____
_____
_____
_____
_____
_____
_____
_____
_____
_____
_____
_____

Engineering Journal (Continued)

Appendix A   Answers to the CCNA Exam Review Questions

Chapter 1
1. b
2. b
3. a
4. b
5. c
6. d
7. c
8. d
9. d
10. c
11. a
12. b
13. a
14. d
15. d

Chapter 2
1. a
2. d
3. c
4. d
5. d
6. a
7. b
8. c
9. d
10. b
11. c
12. d
13. d
14. b
15. a

Chapter 3
1. a
2. d
3. b
4. d
5. b
6. b
7. a
8. c
9. a

10. a
11. a
12. c

Chapter 4
1. c
2. b
3. a
4. b
5. d
6. c
7. a
8. b
9. a
10. b
11. d
12. b
13. c
14. d
15. c
16. a
17. d
18. c
19. d
20. b
21. d
22. c
23. b
24. d
25. a
26. c
27. d
28. b
29. c
30. d
31. a

Chapter 5
1. c
2. b
3. a
4. d
5. c

6. a
7. b

Chapter 6
1. b
2. d
3. b
4. d
5. b
6. d
7. a
8. b
9. c
10. a
11. b
12. c
13. d
14. a
15. d

Chapter 7
1. d
2. a
3. a
4. c
5. d
6. c
7. b
8. c
9. d
10. c
11. a
12. a
13. d

Chapter 8
1. c
2. a
3. b
4. c
5. d
6. a
7. b

8. d
9. b

Chapter 9
1. a
2. d
3. d
4. c
5. b
6. c
7. d
8. a
9. c
10 c
11. a
12. b
13. d
14. c
15. c
16. b
17. b
18. c
19. c
20. a
21. b
22. a
23. b
24. c
25. c
26. d
27. a
28. d
29. c
30. d
31. c
32. a

Chapter 10
1. c
2. b
3. a
4. b
5. c
6. a
7. b
8. d

9. a
10. a
11. b
12. d
13. b
14. a
15. b

Chapter 11
1. a
2. b
3. d
4. d
5. c
6. d
7. a
8. c
9. a
10. a
11. b
12. c
13. c
14. a
15. c
16. a
17. b
18. c

Chapter 12
1. d
2. b
3. c
4. d
5. c
6. d
7. c
8. d
9. c
10. b
11. a
12. b

Chapter 13
1. c
2. a

Chapter 14
1. b
2. b
3. c
4. d
5. b
6. a

Chapter 15
1. a
2. b
3. a
4. c
5. c

Chapter 16
1. a
2. b
3. c
4. d
5. b
6. d
7. d
8. a
9. c
10. d
11. a
12. b
13. d
14. c
15. c
16. d
17. b
18. d
19. a
20. d
21. a
22. b
23. c
24. c
25. c
26. a
27. d

Chapter 17
1. a
2. c
3. a
4. c
5. d
6. a
7. b
8. a
9. c
10. d
11. a
12. b
13. d
14. c
15. a
16. c
17. d
18. b

Chapter 18
1. a
2. b
3. b
4. c
5. b
6. c
7. c
8. d
9. b
10. b
11. a
12. c
13. b
14. d
15. b
16. c
17. a
18. c
19. c
20. c
21. d
22. b
23. c
24. d
25. a

26. c
27. b
28. c
29. a
30. d
31. b
32. b
33. c

Chapter 19
1. b
2. c
3. c
4. a
5. d
6. a
7. a
8. c
9. d
10. a
11. d
12. d
13. b
14. b
15. c
16. a
17. d
18. c
19. c
20. b

Chapter 20
1. b
2. b
3. d
4. a
5. d
6. a
7. c
8. b
9. a
10. a
11. c
12. c
13. d
14. b

15. d
16. c
17. b
18. c
19. d
20. b
21. d
22. a
23. c
24. c
25. a
26. b
27. c
28. c
29. d
30. b

Chapter 21
1. a
2. c
3. d
4. b
5. c
6. c
7. a
8. c
9. b
10. c
11. b
12. a
13. d
14. c
15. d
16. b
17. c
18. a
19. c
20. d

Chapter 22
1. a
2. b
3. a
4. b
5. c

Chapter 23
1. a
2. b
3. c
4. b
5. c
6. d
7. d
8. c
9. d
10. b
11. c
12. c
13. a
14. b
15. c
16. d
17. a
18. b
19. d
20. b

Chapter 24
1. b
2. c
3. b
4. a
5. a
6. d
7. a
8. c
9. a
10. b
11. b
12. d
13. b
14. c
15. d
16. a
17. c
18. a
19. c
20. d
21. d
22. b

Chapter 25
1. b
2. c
3. d
4. d
5. a
6. b
7. a
8. b
9. c
10. a
11. b
12. a
13. c
14. c
15. b
16. a
17. b
18. c
19. d
20. a
21. c
22. d
23. c
24. a
25. b
26. a
27. b
28. c
29. d
30. a
31. a
32. b
33. a
34. d
35. d
36. a
37. b
38. d
39. c
40. a
41. d
42. a
43. b
44. d
45. c

46. d
47. a
48. b
49. c
50. d
51. a
52. b
53. c
54. a
55. d
56. b
57. c
58. d
59. d
60. a
61. b
62. c
63. b
64. c
65. d
66. a
67. b
68. c
69. d
70. a
71. b
72. c
73. a

Chapter 26
1. c
2. d
3. b
4. c
5. b
6. c
7. a
8. c
9. b
10. c
11. b
12. b

Notes

Notes